THE EASY WAY TO LEARN JAPANESE QUICKLY

JAPANESE FOR FUN

PHRASEBOOK & DICTIONARY

Taeko Kamiya

Revised by **Shimomura Kazuhisa**

T0354229

TUTTLE Publishing

Tokyo | Rutland, Vermont | Singapore

Contents

Foreword

ORIGIN OF THE JAPANESE LANGUAGE

Where did the Japanese spoken language come from? No one knows for sure. Some feel there's a strong connection with the Altaic languages of Central Asia. Others believe Japanese is derived from the languages of Southeast Asia and Polynesia. And a few insist that Japanese has no connections at all with any other language.

The writing system, on the other hand, came from China in the sixth century. At that time, Buddhism was being introduced from China, and a writing system was necessary to propagate the wisdom of the sutras.

JAPANESE FOR FUN

This pocket book is intended for people who want to learn Japanese quickly. Whenever you have a few free minutes—waiting in a hotel lobby, riding on a train, or wherever—open this book and you can learn phrases you'll use again and again during your stay in Japan. The book is divided into 22 chapters, each covering a specific topic. Each chapter includes the following three sections:

Words & Expressions: This section introduces words and expressions needed in specific situations. The vocabulary is presented systematically for quick and easy understanding. Simple sentences using the words and expressions are provided under the title "Examples".

Expressions in Context: This shows how to use the words and expressions given in the preceding section within the context. The "Mini Dialogues", sometimes followed by "Other Expressions", is aimed at giving you confidence to use new words in sentences.

Additional Words & Expressions: By providing more words and expressions related to the topic of each chapter, this section enables you to create many new sentences using the patterns just learned and increase your vocabulary. Simple sentences under the title "Examples" will also show you how to use the vocabulary in daily situations. There's no need to memorize all the words or phrases presented here; concentrate on just those you want to use.

Start by reading the first three chapters of the book. These introduce many of the most commonly used words and phrases, and familiarize you with the basic sentence structures. After Chapter 3, go straight to any chapter that interests you. If you want to know what to say on the phone, read Chapter 14; if you have to take a train, a few minutes with Chapter 9 should be able to help you get to your destination with ease.

This book contains a total of over 300 carefully selected words and expressions. There is very little grammar included and there is no need for hours of rote memorization. All that is required is a few minutes of your time.

One final word of advice: do not be afraid to use what you learn. Only by taking the initiative and speaking regularly can you experience the joy of communicating in a foreign language. We hope you'll discover how fun and easy speaking Japanese can be.

Taeko Kamiya

Pronunciation

VOWELS

The Japanese language has five vowels: **a, i, u, e,** and **o**. The vowels are pronounced as follows:

a as in f<u>a</u>ther
i as in <u>ea</u>t
u as in r<u>u</u>le
e as in m<u>e</u>t
o as in s<u>o</u>lo

In spoken Japanese, the **i** and **u** vowel sounds are often weak. This occurs in words like **shika** (deer), which may sound like **shka**, or **desu**, which may sound like **dess**.
   Long vowels are pronounced twice as long as regular vowels and are marked **ā, ū, ē** and **ō**. In this book the double **ii** is used instead of a macron.

CONSONANTS

Most Japanese consonants are pronounced like English consonants. One exception is the Japanese **r**, which sounds like a combination of the English **r** and **l**.
   As shown in the following table, each consonant is followed by a vowel, by a **y** and a vowel, or by an **h** and a vowel. Each syllable is clearly pronounced; thus **haru** (spring) is **ha-ru; kyaku** (customer) is **kya-ku;** and **shumi** (hobby) is **shu-mi**.

When **n** is followed by a vowel within a word, an apostrophe is used to show the break between syllables. Examples of this include **kin'en** (non-smoking) and **man'in** (no vacancy).

Double consonants (**kk, pp, ss, tt**) are pronounced as follows: **Nikko** (a famous tourist spot) like the **k** sound in "book-keeper"; **rippa** (fine) like the **p** sound in "top part"; **issō** (more) like the **s** sound in "less sleep"; **kitte** (stamp) like the **t** sound in "hot tub".

Here is a table of all the sounds in Japanese. It is recommended that you practice the sounds aloud at least two or three times.

TABLE OF SOUNDS IN JAPANESE

a	i	u	e	o
ka	ki	ku	ke	ko
ga	gi	gu	ge	go
sa	shi	su	se	so
za	ji	zu	ze	zo
ta	chi	tsu	te	to
tsa*	ti*	tu*	tse*	tso*
da	di*	du*/dyu*	de	do
na	ni	nu	ne	no
ha	hi	fu	he	ho
ba	bi	bu	be	bo
pa	pi	pu	pe	po

a	i	u	e	o
fa*	fi*	—	fe*	fo*
ma	mi	mu	me	mo
ya	—	yu	—	yo
ra	ri	ru	re	ro
wa	—	—	—	—
n	—	—	—	—
kya	—	kyu	—	kyo
gya	—	gyu	—	gyo
sha	—	shu	she*	sho
ja	—	ju	je*	jo
cha	—	chu	che*	cho
nya	—	nyu	—	nyo
hya	—	hyu/fyu*	—	hyo
bya	—	byu	—	byo
pya	—	pyu	—	pyo
mya	—	myu	—	myo
rya	—	ryu	—	ryo

* These sounds are used only in loanwords, that is, words derived from other languages.

PITCH

Japanese pronunciation is not very difficult once you get used to putting a vowel after every consonant, except "n." What might puzzle learners is the difference between its high and low pitches. For example, when you say, **hashi**, pronouncing **ha** with a high pitch and **shi** with a low pitch, it means "chopsticks" (**ha<u>shi</u>**), whereas if the pitches are the other way round, it means a "bridge" or an "edge" (**ha<u>shi</u>**). Listen to the audio recordings, and follow the native speakers' pitch as closely as you can.

For e.g.

> **Good morning.**
> **<u>Ohayō</u> <u>gozaimahss</u>.**
> おはようございます。

How to access the audio recordings for this book:

1. You must have an Internet connection.
2. Type the URL below into your web browser.

https://www.tuttlepublishing.com/japanese-for-fun-phrasebook-dictionary-audio

For support email us at info@tuttlepublishing.com.

A Few Words About Japanese Grammar

It is not the purpose of this book to explain Japanese grammar. However, it is probably worthwhile to point out a few basic differences between Japanese and English to help you have a better idea of how the sentences are formed.

1. Japanese verbs come at the end of a sentence.

   e.g., **Watashi wa biiru o nomimahss.** (I drink beer or literally, "I beer drink".)

2. Japanese nouns generally do not have plural forms. The noun **kodomo**, for example, can mean either "child" or "children".

3. Articles and some common English adjectives are not used in Japanese. There are no Japanese equivalents for words like "a", "the", "some", and "any".

4. The subject of a sentence, especially **watashi** (I) and **anata** (you), is often dropped.

5. The same verb form is used for both the present and future tenses.

   e.g., **Watashi wa ikimahss.** (I go./I will go.)

6. Three important Japanese particles have no equivalents in English.

   Wa follows the topic or subject of a sentence.

   > e.g., **Watashi wa Honda dess.** (I am Honda.)

   Ga follows the subject of a sentence.

   > e.g., **Hoteru ga arimahss.** (There is a hotel.)

   Wo follows the direct object of a verb.

   > e.g., **Biiru wo nomimahss.** (I drink beer.)

7. Adding the word **ka** to the end of a sentence makes it a question.

   e.g., **Kore wa hoteru dess ka?** (Is this a hotel?)

Good evening.
Konbanwa.
こんばんは。
I'm Smith.
Sumisu dess.
スミスです。
How are you?
O-genki dess ka?
お元気（げんき）ですか？

(I'm) fine.
Hai, genki dess.
はい、元気（げんき）です。
I'm Honda.
Honda dess.
本田（ほんだ）です。
I'm glad to meet you.
Dōzo yoroshiku.
どうぞよろしく。

I'm pleased
to meet you.
Dōzo yoroshiku.
どうぞよろしく。

What's your occupation?
O-shigoto wa?
お仕事（しごと）は？

I don't understand.
Wakarimasen.
わかりません。
Sorry. My Japanese is poor.
Sumimasen. Nihon-go ga heta dess.
すみません。日本語（にほんご）がへたです。
Please say it once more.
Mō ichido itte kudasai.
もう一度（いちど）、言（い）ってください。

CHAPTER 1
Basic Expressions

You'll use these basic expressions again and again during your stay in Japan. If you can, practice them aloud. It'll take you only a few moments to learn them, and when you do, you'll have taken the first and most important step to speaking Japanese.

WORDS & EXPRESSIONS

Good morning.
Ohayō gozaimahss.
おはようございます。

Hello./Good afternoon.
Konnichiwa.
こんにちは。

Good evening.
Konbanwa.
こんばんは。

Good night.
Oyasumi-nasai.
おやすみなさい。

Goodbye.
Sayōnara.
さようなら。

See you later.
Dewa mata.
では、また。

Congratulations.
Omedetō gozaimahss.
おめでとうございます。

Thank you.
Dōmo arigatō./Arigatō.
どうもありがとう。／
ありがとう。

You're welcome.
Dō-itashimashite.
どういたしまして。

[honorific prefix]
o-
お

healthy; fine
genki
元気 (げんき)

yes
hai
はい

no
iie
いいえ

Japanese (language)
Nihon-go
日本語 (にほんご)

Excuse me.
Sumimasen.
すみません。

(honorific added to another person's
name; not used with your own name)
-san
さん

English
Ei-go
英語 (えいご)

EXAMPLES:

How are you?
O-genki dess ka?
お元気 (げんき) ですか?

(I'm) fine.
Hai, genki dess.
はい、元気 (げんき) です。

How do you do?
Hajimemashite.
はじめまして。
(used only when you are
introduced to someone)

Glad to meet you.
Dōzo yoroshiku.
どうぞ、よろしく。
(You can use this in reply as well, or
see the next phrase for another version).

Glad to meet you, too.
Kochira koso (yoroshiku).
こちらこそ (よろしく) 。

What's your name?
O-namae wa?
お名前 (なまえ) は?

What's your occupation?
O-shigoto wa?
お仕事 (しごと) は?

Do you understand English?
Ei-go ga wakarimahss ka?
英語 (えいご) がわかりますか?

I understand.
Wakarimahss.
わかります。

I don't understand.
Wakarimasen.
わかりません。

I don't understand Japanese.
Nihon-go wa wakarimasen.
日本語 (にほんご) はわかりません。

I'm poor at...	I'm poor at Japanese./My Japanese is poor.
heta dess	**Nihon-go ga heta dess.**
へたです	日本語 (にほんご) がへたです。

Mr./Mrs./Ms./Miss Honda
Honda-san
本田 (ほんだ) さん

HOW TO BOW

Bowing properly takes practice, and many companies, especially hotels and department stores, spend considerable time training new employees to do it correctly. The secret to good bowing? Keep your back straight and bend from the hip. Your feet should be placed together and your hands at your sides or clasped in front. Bow deliberately, without rushing. If you don't know what to say as you bow, say **Dōmo**, a phrase that's appropriate for most occasions. One exception is when you're paying respects to the deceased, where you should just keep silent.

EXPRESSIONS IN CONTEXT

 **MINI DIALOGUE 1**

A: Good afternoon, Mr. Honda.
Honda-san, konnichiwa.
本田 (ほんだ) さん、こんにちは。

B: Good afternoon, Mrs. Smith.
Sumisu-san, konnichiwa.
スミスさん、こんにちは。

A: How do you do? I'm Smith. I'm glad to meet you.
Hajimemashite. Sumisu dess. Dōzo yoroshiku.
はじめまして。スミスです。どうぞよろしく。

B: How do you do? I'm Honda. I'm pleased to meet you.
Hajimemashite. Honda dess. Dōzo yoroshiku.
はじめまして。本田 (ほんだ) です。どうぞよろしく。

 MINI DIALOGUE 2

A: How are you?
O-genki dess ka?
お元気 (げんき) ですか?

B: Yes, (I'm) fine.
Hai, genki dess.
はい、元気 (げんき) です。

 MINI DIALOGUE 3

A: Thank you.
Dōmo arigatō.
どうもありがとう。

B: You're welcome.
Dō-itashimashite.
どういたしまして。

MINI DIALOGUE 4

A: Do you understand?
Wakarimahss ka?
わかりますか?

B: Yes, I understand.
Hai, wakarimahss.
はい、わかります。

OTHER EXPRESSIONS

No, I don't understand.
Iie, wakarimasen.
いいえ、わかりません。

Please say it once more.
Mō ichido itte kudasai.
もう一度 (いちど)、言 (い) ってください。

Please speak in English.
Ei-go de hanashite kudasai.
英語 (えいご) で話 (はな) してください。

Please speak slowly.
Yukkuri hanashite kudasai.
ゆっくり話 (はな) してください。

slowly
yukkuri
ゆっくり

LANGUAGES

Vietnamese
Betonamu-go
ベトナム語 (ご)

Chinese
Chūgoku-go
中国語 (ちゅうごくご)

German
Doitsu-go
ドイツ語 (ご)

French
Furansu-go
フランス語 (ご)

Indonesian
Indoneshia-go
インドネシア語 (ご)

Italian
Itaria-go
イタリア語 (ご)

Korean
Kankoku-go
韓国語 (かんこくご)

Portuguese
Porutogaru-go
ポルトガル語 (ご)

Russian
Roshia-go
ロシア語 (ご)

Spanish
Supein-go
スペイン語 (ご)

Thai
Tai-go
タイ語 (ご)

CHAPTER 2
What's What

Over half of what we say in English is made up of fewer than fifty words. It's the same in Japanese. Just by learning the following words and phrases, you'll be able to make hundreds of different sentences. And remember, to make a question, add **-ka** to the end of a sentence with a rising intonation.

WORDS & EXPRESSIONS

this
kore
これ

[subject particle]
wa
は

Shinto shrine
jinja
神社 (じんじゃ)

is; am; are
dess
です

that
are
あれ

Buddhist temple
o-tera
お寺 (てら)

the Kabuki Theater
Kabuki-za
歌舞伎座 (かぶきざ)

Kabuki
Kabuki
歌舞伎 (かぶき)

yes
hai
はい

that's right
sō dess
そうです

no
iie
いいえ

isn't; am not; aren't
dewa arimasen
ではありません

woodblock print
hanga
版画 (はんが)

what
nan(i)
何 (なん、なに)

Shinto shrine archway
torii
鳥居 (とりい)

the Imperial Palace
Kōkyo
皇居（こうきょ）

castle
o-shiro
お城（しろ）

bonsai (miniature pot-
ted tree or shrub)
bonsai
盆栽（ぼんさい）

wind chime
fūrin
風鈴（ふうりん）

EXAMPLES

This is a Shinto shrine.
Kore wa jinja dess.
これは神社（じんじゃ）です。

Is that the Kabuki Theater?
Are wa Kabuki-za dess ka?
あれは歌舞伎座（かぶきざ）ですか？

What's this?
Kore wa nan dess ka?
これは何（なん）ですか？

Is this the Imperial Palace?
Kore wa Kōkyo dess ka?
これは皇居（こうきょ）ですか？

This is a bonsai.
Kore wa bonsai dess.
これは盆栽（ぼんさい）です。

That is a Buddhist temple.
Are wa o-tera dess.
あれはお寺（てら）です。

Yes, it is.
Hai, sō dess.
はい、そうです。

This is a Shinto shrine archway.
Kore wa torii dess.
これは鳥居（とりい）です。

Is that a castle?
Are wa o-shiro dess ka?
あれはお城（しろ）ですか？

That isn't a wind chime.
Are wa fūrin dewa arimasen.
あれは風鈴（ふうりん）ではありません。

SHRINES AND TEMPLES

What's the difference between a shrine and a temple? Shrines are worship grounds for Shinto, a religion that originated in Japan. Temples are places of worship for Buddhism, which originally came from India. In some places in Japan, shrines and temples stand side by side.

A shrine can be identified by a **torii,** an arch made of two crossbeams supported by two pillars. The **torii** represents the union of man and woman and marks the entrance to the shrine grounds. At a temple, you can always find a statue of a Buddha inside one of the buildings.

EXPRESSIONS IN CONTEXT

 MINI DIALOGUE 1

A: What's this?
  Kore wa nan dess ka?
  これは何（なん）ですか？

B: This is a Buddhist temple.
  O-tera dess.
  お寺（てら）です。

OTHER EXPRESSIONS

This is a statue of a Buddha.
Kore wa Butsuzō dess.
これは仏像（ぶつぞう）です。

This is the main sanctuary of the shrine.
Kore ga honden dess.
これが本殿（ほんでん）です。

 **MINI DIALOGUE 2**

A: What's that?
Are wa nan dess ka?
あれは何 (なん) ですか？

B: That's the Kabuki Theater.
Are wa Kabuki-za dess.
あれは歌舞伎座 (かぶきざ) です。

OTHER EXPRESSIONS

That's the Imperial Palace.
Are wa Kōkyo dess.
あれは皇居 (こうきょ) です。

That's a castle.
Are wa o-shiro dess.
あれはお城 (しろ) です。

 **MINI DIALOGUE 3**

A: Is this a woodblock print?
Kore wa hanga dess ka?
これは版画 (はんが) ですか？

B: Yes, it is.
Hai, sō dess.
はい、そうです。

OTHER EXPRESSIONS

No, it's not a woodblock print.
Iie, hanga dewa arimasen.
いいえ、版画 (はんが) ではありません。

 **MINI DIALOGUE 4**

A: Is this a bonsai?
Kore wa bonsai dess ka?
これは盆栽 (ぼんさい) ですか？

B: No, it's not a bonsai.
Iie, bonsai dewa arimasen.
いいえ、盆栽 (ぼんさい) ではありません。

GEOGRAPHICAL TERMS

mountain
yama
山 (やま)

ocean
umi
海 (うみ)

prefecture
ken
県 (けん)

plain; open field
heiya
平野 (へいや)

the Pacific Ocean
Taihei-yō
太平洋 (たいへいよう)

Hiroshima Prefecture
Hiroshima-ken *See
"PREFECTURES IN JAPAN"
広島県 (ひろしまけん)

river
kawa
川 (かわ)

the Sea of Japan
Nihon-kai
日本海 (にほんかい)

lake
mizuumi
湖 (みずうみ)

Inland Sea
Seto-naikai
瀬戸内海 (せとないかい)

SIGHTSEEING

town; city
machi
町 (まち)

temple gate
sanmon
山門 (さんもん)

botanical garden
shokubutsu-en
植物園 (しょくぶつえん)

country; rural area
inaka
田舎 (いなか)

museum
hakubutsu-kan
博物館 (はくぶつかん)

amusement park
yūen-chi
遊園地 (ゆうえんち)

pagoda; tower
tō
塔 (とう)

art museum
bijutsu-kan
美術館 (びじゅつかん)

Ueno Park
Ueno Kōen
上野公園 (うえのこうえん)

statue of a Buddha
butsuzō
仏像 (ぶつぞう)

zoo
dōbutsu-en
動物園 (どうぶつえん)

station
eki
駅 (えき)

Tokyo Station
Tōkyō Eki
東京駅 (とうきょうえき)

Tokyo Tower
Tōkyō Tawā
東京 (とうきょう) タワー

Imperial Hotel
Teikoku Hoteru
帝国 (ていこく) ホテル

tea field
cha-batake
茶畑 (ちゃばたけ)

oyster bed (cultivated)
kaki-yōshokujō
牡蠣養殖場 (かきようしょくじょう)

rice paddy
suiden
水田 (すいでん)

AROUND TOWN

road
dōro
道路 (どうろ)

expressway
kōsoku-dōro
高速道路 (こうそくどうろ)

street
michi
道 (みち)

building
biru
ビル

skyscraper
kōsō-biru
高層 (こうそう) ビル

hotel
hoteru
ホテル

PREFECTURES IN JAPAN

Hokkaidō Area
Hokkaidō
北海道 (ほっかいどう)

Tōhoku Area
Aomori-ken
青森県 (あおもりけん)

Iwate-ken
岩手県 (いわてけん)

Miyagi-ken
宮城県 (みやぎけん)

Akita-ken
秋田県 (あきたけん)

Yamagata-ken
山形県 (やまがたけん)

Fukushima-ken
福島県 (ふくしまけん)

Kantō Area
Ibaraki-ken
茨城県 (いばらきけん)

Tochigi-ken
栃木県 (とちぎけん)

Gunma-ken
群馬県 (ぐんまけん)

Saitama-ken
埼玉県 (さいたまけん)

Chiba-ken
千葉県 (ちばけん)

Tōkyō-to
東京都 (とうきょうと)

Kanagawa-ken
神奈川県 (かながわけん)

Kyūshū/Okinawa Area
Fukuoka-ken
福岡県 (ふくおかけん)

Saga-ken
佐賀県 (さがけん)

Nagasaki-ken
長崎県 (ながさきけん)

Kumamoto-ken
熊本県 (くまもとけん)

Ōita-ken
大分県 (おおいたけん)

Miyazaki-ken
宮崎県 (みやざきけん)

Kagoshima-ken
鹿児島県 (かごしまけん)

Okinawa-ken
沖縄県 (おきなわけん)

Chūbu Area
Niigata-ken
新潟県 (にいがたけん)

Toyama-ken
富山県 (とやまけん)

Ishikawa-ken
石川県 (いしかわけん)

Fukui-ken
福井県 (ふくいけん)

Yamanashi-ken
山梨県 (やまなしけん)

Nagano-ken
長野県 (ながのけん)

Gifu-ken
岐阜県 (ぎふけん)

Shizuoka-ken
静岡県 (しずおかけん)

Aichi-ken
愛知県 (あいちけん)

Mie-ken
三重県 (みえけん)

Kansai Area
Shiga-ken
滋賀県 (しがけん)

Kyōto-fu
京都府 (きょうとふ)

Ōsaka-fu
大阪府 (おおさかふ)

Hyōgo-ken
兵庫県 (ひょうごけん)

Nara-ken
奈良県 (ならけん)

Wakayama-ken
和歌山県 (わかやまけん)

Chūgoku Area
Tottori-ken
鳥取県 (とっとりけん)

Shimane-ken
島根県 (しまねけん)

Okayama-ken
岡山県 (おかやまけん)

Hiroshima-ken
広島県 (ひろしまけん)

Yamaguchi-ken
山口県 (やまぐちけん)

Shikoku Area
Tokushima-ken
徳島県 (とくしまけん)

Kagawa-ken
香川県 (かがわけん)

Ehime-ken
愛媛県 (えひめけん)

Kōchi-ken
高知県 (こうちけん)

CHAPTER 3

Introducing Yourself

Polite speech in Japanese can be very complicated and is based on being respectful when referring to others and humble when referring to yourself. Don't worry about polite speech too much though, just remember to attach **-san** to other people's names and not to use it with yours.

WORDS & EXPRESSIONS

I **watashi** 私 (わたし)	Mr./Mrs./Ms./Miss Tanaka **Tanaka-san** 田中 (たなか) さん	person **hito** 人 (ひと)
Smith **Sumisu** スミス	[question particle] **ka** か	that person **ano hito** あの人 (ひと)
is; am; are **dess** です	isn't; am not; are not **dewa arimasen** ではありません	who **dare** 誰 (だれ)
American (person) **Amerika-jin** アメリカ人 (じん)	Japanese (person) **Nihon-jin** 日本人 (にほんじん)	my **watashi no** 私 (わたし) の
you **anata** あなた	that **ano** あの	father (one's own father) **chichi** 父 (ちち)

| Mr./Mrs./Ms./Miss Tanaka's
Tanaka-san no
田中 (たなか) さんの | father (someone else's father;
also used when addressing one's
own father)
otō-san
お父 (とう) さん | your
anata no
あなたの

name
namae
名前 (なまえ) |

EXAMPLES

My name is Smith. (lit., I'm Smith.)
Watashi wa Sumisu dess.
私 (わたし) はスミスです。

I'm an American.
Watashi wa Amerika-jin dess.
私 (わたし) はアメリカ人 (じん) です。

Are you Mr. Tanaka?
Anata wa Tanaka-san dess ka?
あなたは田中 (たなか) さんですか？

That's right.
Sō dess.
そうです。

No, I'm not.
Chigaimahss.
違 (ちが) います。

I'm not Tanaka.
Watashi wa Tanaka dewa arimasen.
私 (わたし) は田中 (たなか) ではありません。

What's your name?
Anata no o-namae wa?
あなたのお名前 (なまえ) は？

Who's that person?
Ano hito wa dare dess ka?
あの人 (ひと) は誰 (だれ) ですか？

He's my father.
Watashi no chichi dess.
私 (わたし) の父 (ちち) です。

He's Mr. Tanaka's father.
Tanaka-san no otō-san dess.
田中 (たなか) さんのお父 (とう) さんです。

POLITE COMPLICATIONS

Many new employees spend their first days on the job learning when to use honorific and humble speech. It can be confusing at first. For example, suppose a new employee is talking to the company president. He'll be using as many honorifics as he can. The phone rings. The young man picks it up and the caller is looking for the president, Mr. Sato. "Sato is not in." the young man says using humble speech to refer to his president. Rude? Far from it. He's merely showing respect to the caller, someone outside his company, by using humble speech to refer to a member of his own company, even if that person's (in this case, Mr. Sato) status is much higher than his.

EXPRESSIONS IN CONTEXT

 **MINI DIALOGUE 1**

A: Are you Mr. Smith?
Anata wa Sumisu-san dess ka?
あなたはスミスさんですか？

B: Yes, I am.
Hai, sō dess.
はい、そうです。

OTHER EXPRESSIONS

No, I'm not.
Iie, chigaimahss.
いいえ、違 (ちが) います。

A: What's your name?
Anata no o-namae wa?
あなたのお名前（なまえ）は？

B: My name is Smith.
Watashi wa Sumisu dess.
私（わたし）はスミスです。

A: Are you Japanese?
Anata wa Nihon-jin dess ka?
あなたは日本人（にほんじん）ですか？

B: I'm an American.
Watashi wa Amerika-jin dess.
私（わたし）はアメリカ人（じん）です。

OTHER EXPRESSIONS

Are you an American?
Anata wa Amerika-jin dess ka?
あなたはアメリカ人（じん）ですか？

I'm not Japanese.
Watashi wa Nihon-jin dewa arimasen.
私（わたし）は日本人（にほんじん）ではありません。

A: Who's that person?
Ano hito wa dare dess ka?
あの人（ひと）は誰（だれ）ですか？

B: That's Mr. Tanaka.
Tanaka-san dess.
田中（たなか）さんです。

OTHER EXPRESSIONS

Is that person Mrs. Tanaka's father?
Ano hito wa Tanaka-san no otō-san dess ka?
あの人 (ひと) は田中 (たなか) さんのお父 (とう) さですか？

That person isn't Mr. Tanaka.
Ano hito wa Tanaka-san dewa arimasen.
あの人 (ひと) は田中 (たなか) さんではありません。

That person isn't my father.
Ano hito wa watashi no chichi dewa arimasen.
あの人 (ひと) は私 (わたし) の父 (ちち) ではありません。

NATIONS AND NATIONALITIES

The United States
Amerika
アメリカ

American
Amerika-jin
アメリカ人

Vietnam
Betonamu
ベトナム

Vietnamese
Betonamu-jin
ベトナム人 (じん)

China
Chūgoku
中国 (ちゅうごく)

Chinese
Chūgoku-jin
中国人 (ちゅうごくじん)

France
Furansu
フランス

French
Furansu-jin
フランス人 (じん)

Great Britain/the United Kingdom
Igirisu
イギリス

British
Igirisu-jin
イギリス人 (じん)

Italy
Itaria
イタリア

Italian
Itaria-jin
イタリア人 (じん)

Canada
Kanada
カナダ

Canadian
Kanada-jin
カナダ人 (じん)

Korea (ROK)
Kankoku
韓国 (かんこく)

Korean
Kankoku-jin
韓国人 (かんこくじん)

Germany
Doitsu
ドイツ

German
Doitsu-jin
ドイツ人 (じん)

Australia
Ōsutoraria
オーストラリア

Australian
Ōsutoraria-jin
オーストラリア人 (じん)

Portugal
Porutogaru
ポルトガル

Portuguese
Porutogaru-jin
ポルトガル人 (じん)

Russia
Roshia
ロシア

Russian
Roshia-jin
ロシア人 (じん)

Spain
Supein
スペイン

Spanish
Supein-jin
スペイン人 (じん)

OCCUPATIONS

teacher
sensei
先生 (せんせい)

secretary
hisho
秘書 (ひしょ)

lawyer
bengo-shi
弁護士 (べんごし)

student
gakusei
学生 (がくせい)

company employee
kaisha-in
会社員 (かいしゃいん)

reporter; journalist
kisha
記者 (きしゃ)

RELATIVES

father (someone else's
father or father-in-law)
otō-san
お父さん

older brother (someone
else's older brother or
brother-in-law)
onii-san
お兄 (にい) さん

younger brother (some-
one else's younger brother
or brother-in-law)
otōto-san
弟 (おとうと) さん

mother (one's own mother
or mother-in-law)
haha
母 (はは)

older sister (one's older
sister or sister-in-law)
ane
姉 (あね)

younger sister (one's
own younger sister or
sister-in-law)
imōto
妹 (いもうと)

mother (someone else's
mother or mother-in-law)
okā-san
お母 (かあ) さん

older sister (someone
else's older sister or
sister-in-law)
onē-san
お姉 (ねえ) さん

younger sister (someone
else's younger sister or
sister-in-law)
imōto-san
妹 (いもうと) さん

older brother (one's own
older brother or brother-
in-law)
ani
兄 (あに)

younger brother (one's
own younger brother)
otōto
弟 (おとうと)

son (one's own son or son-in-law)
musuko
息子 (むすこ)

son (someone else's son or son-in-law)
musuko-san
息子 (むすこ) さん

daughter (one's own daughter or daughter-in-law)
musume
娘 (むすめ)

daughter (someone else's daughter or daughter-in-law)
musume-san
娘 (むすめ) さん

grandchild (one's own grandchild)
mago
孫 (まご)

grandchild (someone else's grandchild)
omago-san
お孫 (まご) さん

husband (one's husband)
otto
夫 (おっと)

husband (someone else's husband)
danna-san
だんなさん

wife (one's wife)
kanai
家内

wife (someone else's wife)
oku-san
奥 (おく) さん

aunt (one's own aunt)
oba
おば

aunt (someone else's aunt)
oba-san
おばさん

uncle (one's own uncle)
oji
おじ

uncle (someone else's uncle)
oji-san
おじさん

OTHERS

friend
tomodachi
友 (とも) だち

he
kare
彼 (かれ)

she
kanojo
彼女 (かのじょ)

child
kodomo
子 (こ) ども

adult
otona
大人 (おとな)

female
onna
女 (おんな)

male
otoko
男 (おとこ)

girl
onna no ko
女 (おんな) の子 (こ)

boy
otoko no ko
男 (おとこ) の子 (こ)

woman
onna no hito
女 (おんな) の人 (ひと)

man
otoko no hito
男 (おとこ) の人 (ひと)

CHAPTER 4
Numbers

For counting ten objects or less, use the numbers presented below. For example, if you want six folding fans, say **Sensu wo muttsu kudasai**. If you have four bags, say **Nimotsu ga yottsu arimahss**. The good thing about numbers is that you can always use your fingers to make certain someone understands you.

WORDS & EXPRESSIONS

one (of these)
hitotsu
1つ（ひとつ）

please; please give
kudasai
ください

one of these
**kore wo hitotsu/
kono uchi no hitotsu**
これを1つ（ひとつ）／
このうちのひとつ

sandwich
sandoitchi
サンドイッチ

two
futatsu
2つ（ふたつ）

folding fan
sensu
扇子（せんす）

three
mittsu
3つ（みっつ）

four
yottsu
4つ（よっつ）

five
itsutsu
5つ（いつつ）

six
muttsu
6つ（むっつ）

seven
nanatsu
7つ（ななつ）

eight
yattsu
8つ（やっつ）

nine
kokonotsu
9つ（ここのつ）

ten
tō
10（とお）

ten pieces **jukko** 10個 (じゅっこ)	bag; baggage **nimotsu** 荷物 (にもつ)	many **takusan** たくさん
how many **ikutsu** いくつ	[subject particle] **ga** が	
want/need **irimahss** いります	there is; there are **arimahss** あります	

EXAMPLES

Please give me one.
Hitotsu kudasai.
1つ (ひとつ) ください。

Please give me one of these.
Kore wo hitotsu kudasai.
これを1つ (ひとつ) ください。

Please give me two sandwiches.
Sandoitchi wo futatsu kudasai.
サンドイッチを2つ (ふたつ) ください。

Please give me three folding fans.
Sensu wo mittsu kudasai.
扇子 (せんす) を3つ (みっつ) ください。

How many do you want?
Ikutsu irimasu ka?/ Ikutsu dess ka?
いくついりますか?／いくつですか?

I want ten.
Jukko dess.
10個 (じゅっこ) です。

How many bags are there?
Nimotsu wa ikutsu arimahss ka?
荷物 (にもつ) はいくつありますか?

There are four.
Yottsu arimahss.
4つ (よっつ) あります。

There are many.
Takusan arimahss.
たくさんあります。

I have many bags.
Nimotsu ga takusan arimahss.
荷物 (にもつ) がたくさんあります。

COUNTERS

Another way of counting uses special words that are attached to numerals. These words, called counters, vary according to the type of object. For example, long, thin objects like pens take the counter **hon**; flat objects use **mai**.

Counters exist for cars, fish, birds, buildings, airplanes, clothing, small animals, and large animals. There's even one for Japanese poems, and a different one for Chinese poems. But don't fret about remembering all of them. It's all right to count things with **hitotsu, futatsu, mittsu**, etc.

EXPRESSIONS IN CONTEXT

 MINI DIALOGUE 1

A: Excuse me. Please give me this.
   Sumimasen. Kore wo kudasai.
   すみません。これをください。

A: Five, please.
   Itsutsu, kudasai.
   5つ (いつつ) ください。

B: How many do you want?
   Ikutsu dess ka?
   いくつですか？

OTHER EXPRESSIONS

Please give me two of these.
Kore wo futatsu kudasai.
これを2つ (ふたつ) ください。

Please give me six of these.
Muttsu kudasai.
6つ (むっつ) ください。

Please give me four sandwiches.
Sandoitchi wo yottsu kudasai.
サンドイッチを4つ (よっつ) ください。

Please give me three folding fans.
Sensu wo mittsu kudasai.
扇子 (せんす) を3つ (みっつ) ください。

 MINI DIALOGUE 2

A: How many bags are there?
 Nimotsu wa ikutsu arimahss ka?
 荷物 (にもつ) はいくつありますか?

B: There are seven.
 Nanatsu arimahss.
 7つ (ななつ) あります。

OTHER EXPRESSIONS

There are nine.
Kokonotsu arimahss.
9つ (ここのつ) あります。

 MINI DIALOGUE 3

A: Do you have many folding fans?
 Sensu wa takusan arimahss ka?
 扇子 (せんす) はたくさんありますか?

B: Yes, I have eight.
 Hai, yattsu arimahss.
 はい、8つ (やっつ) あります。

OTHER EXPRESSIONS

No, I have one.
Iie, hitotsu dess.
いいえ、1つ（ひとつ）です。

NUMBERS

The numbers presented here are used for time, prices, rankings, and so forth. These numbers may also be used for counting more than ten objects. Numbers are written either in *kanji* or numerals, but for more than ten *kanji* is rarely used in daily situations, except denominations such as **sen** (thousand) and **man** (ten thousand). However, for your reference, *kanji* are provided for all the numbers in the list below.

1	5	9
ichi	**go**	**ku/kyū**
一（いち）	五（ご）	九（く／きゅう）

2	6	10
ni	**roku**	**jū**
二（に）	六（ろく）	十（じゅう）

3	7	11
san	**shichi/nana**	**jū-ichi**
三（さん）	七（しち／なな）	十一（じゅういち）

4	8	12
shi/yon	**hachi**	**jū-ni**
四（し／よん）	八（はち）	十二（じゅうに）

13
jū-san
十三 (じゅうさん)

14
jū-shi/jū-yon
十四 (じゅうし／
じゅうよん)

15
jū-go
十五 (じゅうご)

16
jū-roku
十六 (じゅうろく)

17
jū-shichi/jū-nana
十七 (じゅうしち／
じゅうなな)

18
jū-hachi
十八 (じゅうはち)

19
jū-ku/jū-kyū
十九 (じゅうく／
じゅうきゅう)

20
ni-jū
二十 (にじゅう)

21
ni-jū-ichi
二十一 (にじゅういち)

30
san-jū
三十 (さんじゅう)

31
san-jū-ichi
三十一 (さんじゅういち)

40
yon-jū
四十 (よんじゅう)

50
go-jū
五十 (ごじゅう)

60
roku-jū
六十 (ろくじゅう)

70
shichi-jū/nana-jū
七十 (しちじゅう／
ななじゅう)

80
hachi-jū
八十 (はちじゅう)

90
kyū-jū
九十 (きゅうじゅう)

100
hyaku
百 (ひゃく)

101
hyaku-ichi
百一 (ひゃくいち)

110
hyaku-jū
百十 (ひゃくじゅう)

200
ni-hyaku
二百 (にひゃく)

300
san-byaku
三百 (さんびゃく)

400
yon-hyaku
四百 (よんひゃく)

500
go-hyaku
五百 (ごひゃく)

600
rop-pyaku
六百 (ろっぴゃく)

700 **nana-hyaku** 七百 (ななひゃく)	3,000 **san-zen** 三千 (さんぜん)	8,000 **has-sen** 八千 (はっせん)
800 **hap-pyaku** 八百 (はっぴゃく)	4,000 **yon-sen** 四千 (よんせん)	9,000 **kyū-sen** 九千 (きゅうせん)
900 **kyū-hyaku** 九百 (きゅうひゃく)	5,000 **go-sen** 五千 (ごせん)	10,000 **ichi-man** 一万 (いちまん)
1,000 **sen** 千 (せん)	6,000 **roku-sen** 六千 (ろくせん)	100,000 **jū-man** 十万 (じゅうまん)
2,000 **ni-sen** 二千 (にせん)	7,000 **nana-sen** 七千 (ななせん)	1,000,000 **hyaku-man** 百万 (ひゃくまん)

EXAMPLES

Please give me a bowl of rice.
Gohan wo ippai kudasai.
ご飯 (はん) を1杯 (いっぱい) ください。

Please give me a plate of sausages.
Sosēiji wo hitosara kudasai.
ソーセージを1皿 (ひとさら) ください。

Please give me twenty of these.
Kore o ni-jū kudasai.
これを20 (にじゅう) ください。

COUNTING PEOPLE

1 person
hitori
1人／一人 (ひとり)

2 people
futari
2人／二人 (ふたり)

[suffix to count more than two people]
-nin
人 (にん)

3 people
san-nin
3人／三人 (さんにん)

4 people
yo-nin
4人／四人 (よにん)

5 people
go-nin
5人／五人 (ごにん)

6 people
roku-nin
6人／六人 (ろくにん)

7 people
shichi-nin/nana-nin
7人／七人 (しちにん／ななにん)

8 people
hachi-nin
8人／八人 (はちにん)

9 people
kyū-nin/ku-nin
9人／九人 (きゅうにん／くにん)

10 people
jū-nin
10人／十人 (じゅうにん)

man
otoko no hito
男 (おとこ) の人 (ひと)

woman
onna no hito
女 (おんな) の人 (ひと)

There are five people.
Hito ga go-nin imahss.
人 (ひと) が5人 (ごにん) います。

NUMBER OF NIGHTS

overnight stay
ip-paku
1泊(いっぱく)

two-night stay
ni-haku
2泊(にはく)

three-night stay
san-paku
3泊(さんぱく)

four-night stay
yon-haku
4泊(よんはく)

five-night stay
go-haku
5泊(ごはく)

six-night stay
rop-paku
6泊(ろっぱく)

seven-night stay
nana-haku
7泊(ななはく)

eight-night stay
hap-paku
8泊(はっぱく)

nine-night stay
kyū-haku
9泊(きゅうはく)

10-night stay
jup-paku/jip-paku
10泊(じゅっぱく／じっぱく)

CHAPTER 5
Telling Time

To tell time, combine the numbers introduced in Chapter 4 (**ichi, ni, san**, etc.) with **ji** (hour) and **fun** (minute). Remember that a.m. is **gozen**, and p.m. is **gogo**. These words go before the time, as in **gozen jū-ji** (10:00 a.m.). Note that in some cases, **fun** changes to **pun**, such as **ippun, sanpun, roppun, happun** and **jippun** (one, three, six, eight and ten minutes respectively).

WORDS & EXPRESSIONS

1:00 **ichi-ji** 1時 (いちじ)	one minute **ip-pun** 1分 (いっぷん)	five minutes **go-fun** 5分 (ごふん)
4:00 **yo-ji** 4時 (よじ)	two minutes **ni-fun** 2分 (にふん)	six minutes **rop-pun** 6分 (ろっぷん)
a.m. **gozen** 午前 (ごぜん)	three minutes **san-pun** 3分 (さんぷん)	seven minutes **nana-fun*** 7分 (ななふん) *Although 7 in Japanese is either **shichi** or **nana**, **shichi-fun** is rarely used.
p.m. **gogo** 午後 (ごご)	four minutes **yon-pun** 4分 (よんぷん)	

eight minutes
hachi-fun/hap-pun
8分 (はちふん／はっぷん)

nine minutes
kyū-fun
9分 (きゅうふん)

ten minutes
jip-pun
10分 (じっぷん)

before
mae
前 (まえ)

half (past)
han
半 (はん)

now
ima
今 (いま)

what time
nan-ji
何時 (なんじ)

what time
nan-ji ni
何時 (なんじ) に

go out; leave
dekakemahss
出 (で) かけます

breakfast
asa-gohan
朝 (あさ) ごはん

supper (dinner)
ban-gohan
晩 (ばん) ごはん

movie
eiga
映画 (えいが)

start
hajimarimahss
始 (はじ) まります

EXAMPLES

It's 1:00.
Ichi-ji dess.
1時 (いちじ) です。

It's 5:10 a.m.
Gozen go-ji jip-pun dess.
午前 (ごぜん) 5時 (ごじ) 10分
(じっぷん) です。

It's 4:00 p.m.
Gogo yo-ji dess.
午後4時 (ごごよじ) です。

10 minutes before 5:00
go-ji jip-pun mae
5時 (ごじ) 10分 (じっぷん) 前 (まえ)

It's 6:30 p.m.
Gogo roku-ji-han dess.
午後（ごご）6時半（ろくじはん）です。

What time is it now?
Ima nan-ji dess ka?
今（いま）何時（なんじ）ですか？

What time shall we go out?
Nan-ji ni dekakemahss ka?
何時（なんじ）に出（で）かけますか？

What time is breakfast?
Asa-gohan wa nan-ji dess ka?
朝（あさ）ごはんは何時（なんじ）ですか？

What time does the movie start?
Eiga wa nan-ji ni hajimarimahss ka?
映画（えいが）は何時（なんじ）に始（はじ）まりますか？

TIME INFORMATION

Trains and planes operate on the 24-hour timetable. Thus, midnight is 00:00, 9 a.m. is 09:00, and 5 p.m. is 17:00. If this is confusing, confirm times using the regular 12-hour method, carefully enunciating **gozen** (a.m.) or **gogo** (p.m.).

All of Japan lies in a single time zone that is one hour behind Sydney, one hour ahead of Hong Kong and Singapore, nine hours ahead of London, and fourteen hours ahead of New York.

EXPRESSIONS IN CONTEXT

 **MINI DIALOGUE 1**

A: What time is it now?
   Ima nan-ji dess ka?
   今 (いま) 何時 (なんじ) ですか?

B: It's 8:00.
   Hachi-ji dess.
   8時 (はちじ) です。

OTHER EXPRESSIONS

It's 7 minutes before 10:00.
Jū-ji nana-fun mae dess.
10時 (じゅうじ) 7分 (ななふん) 前 (まえ) です。

It's 1:30.
Ichi-ji san-jup-pun dess.
1時 (いちじ) 30分 (さんじゅっぷん) です。

It's 2:30.
Ni-ji-han dess.
2時半 (にじはん) です。

It's 9:05.
Ku-ji go-fun dess.
9時 (くじ) 5分 (ごふん) です。

It's 6:25 a.m.
Gozen roku-ji ni-jū-go-fun dess.
午前 (ごぜん) 6時 (ろくじ) 25分 (にじゅうごふん) です。

It's 4:30 p.m.
Gogo yo-ji-han dess.
午後 (ごご) 4時半 (よじはん) です。

 **MINI DIALOGUE 2**

A: What time is supper?
Ban-gohan wa nan-ji dess ka?
晩 (ばん) ごはんは何時 (なんじ) ですか?

B: It's at 7:15.
Shichi-ji jū-go-fun dess.
7時 (しちじ) 15分 (じゅうごふん) です。

 **MINI DIALOGUE 3**

A: What time is the movie?
Eiga wa nan-ji dess ka?
映画 (えいが) は何時 (なんじ) ですか?

B: It's at 3:45.
San-ji yon-jū-go-fun dess.
3時 (さんじ) 45分 (よんじゅうごふん) です。

 **MINI DIALOGUE 4**

A: What time does it start?
Nan-ji ni hajimarimahss ka?
何時 (なんじ) に始 (はじ) まりますか?

B: At 5:20.
Go-ji ni-jup-pun dess.
5時 (ごじ) 20分 (にじゅっぷん) です。

A: What time is the Kabuki performance?
 Kabuki wa nan-ji dess ka?
 歌舞伎 (かぶき) は何時 (なんじ) ですか？

B: It starts at 8:00.
 Hachi-ji ni hajimarimahss.
 8時 (はちじ) に始 (はじ) まります。

A: What time shall we leave?
 Nan-ji ni dekakemahss ka?
 何時 (なんじ) に出 (で) かけますか？

B: We'll leave at 7:30.
 Shichi-ji-han ni dekakemahss.
 7時半 (しちじはん) に出 (で) かけます。

ADDITIONAL WORDS & EXPRESSIONS

meal; cooked rice
gohan
ごはん

tea time
o-cha no jikan
お茶 (ちゃ) の時間 (じかん)

lunch
hiru-gohan
昼 (ひる) ごはん

arrival time
tōchaku-jikan
到着時間 (とうちゃくじかん)

departure time **shuppatsu-jikan** 出発時間 (しゅっぱつじかん)	the time a group disperses **kaisan-jikan** 解散時間 (かいさんじかん)
the time a performance starts **kaien-jikan** 開演時間 (かいえんじかん)	promise; engagement; appointment **yakusoku** 約束 (やくそく)
opening hour of a store **kaiten-jikan** 開店時間 (かいてんじかん)	time set for an appointment **yakusoku no jikan** 約束 (やくそく) の時間 (じかん)
closing hour of a store **heiten-jikan** 閉店時間 (へいてんじかん)	watch; clock **tokei** 時計 (とけい)
meeting time **shūgō-jikan** 集合時間 (しゅうごうじかん)	alarm clock **mezamashi-dokei** 目覚 (めざ) まし時計 (どけい)

EXAMPLES

What time do we depart?
Shuppatsu-jikan wa nan-ji dess ka?
出発時間 (しゅっぱつじかん) は何時 (なんじ) ですか？

Do you have an alarm clock?
Mezamashi-dokei wa arimahss ka?
目覚 (めざ) まし時計 (どけい) はありますか？

CHAPTER 6
Days of the Week

The key to improving your Japanese is to use it every chance you get. Don't be embarrassed and don't get discouraged. One tip: avoid putting strong stresses on the syllables in your sentences. You're much better off speaking in a flat monotone than stressing the wrong syllables.

WORDS & EXPRESSIONS

Today
kyō
今日 (きょう)

tomorrow
ashita
明日 (あした)

yesterday
kinō
昨日 (きのう)

Monday
Getsu-yōbi
月曜日 (げつようび)

Tuesday
Ka-yōbi
火曜日 (かようび)

Wednesday
Sui-yōbi
水曜日 (すいようび)

Thursday
Moku-yōbi
木曜日 (もくようび)

Friday
Kin-yōbi
金曜日 (きんようび)

Saturday
Do-yōbi
土曜日 (どようび)

Sunday
Nichi-yōbi
日曜日 (にちようび)

was; were
deshita
でした

day after tomorrow
asatte
明後日 (あさって)

what day (of the week)	wedding ceremony	farewell party
nan-yōbi	**kekkon-shiki**	**sōbetsu-kai**
何曜日 (なんようび)	結婚式 (けっこんしき)	送別会 (そうべつかい)
holiday; day off	exposition	picnic
yasumi	**hakuran-kai**	**pikunikku**
休み (やすみ)	博覧会 (はくらんかい)	ピクニック
sightseeing	party	field trip; tour of a factory, institution, etc.
kankō	**pātii**	**kengaku-ryokō**
観光 (かんこう)	パーティー	見学旅行 (けんがくりょこう)

EXAMPLES

Today is Monday.
Kyō wa Getsu-yōbi dess.
今日 (きょう) は月曜日 (げつようび) です。

Tomorrow is Tuesday.
Ashita wa Ka-yōbi dess.
明日 (あした) は火曜日 (かようび) です。

Yesterday was Sunday.
Kinō wa Nichi-yōbi deshita.
昨日 (きのう) は日曜日 (にちようび) でした。

What day of the week are we going sightseeing?
Kankō wa nan-yōbi dess ka?
観光 (かんこう) は何曜日 (なんようび) ですか?

When is the party (lit., What day of the week is the party?)
Pātii wa nan-yōbi dess ka?
パーティーは何曜日（なんようび）ですか？

It's (on) Saturday.
Do-yōbi dess.
土曜日（どようび）です。

MEANINGS OF THE DAYS OF THE WEEKS

In Japanese, the days of the week derive from the world of nature. **Getsu-yōbi** (Monday) means "moon day"; **Ka-yōbi** (Tuesday), "fire day"; **Sui-yōbi** (Wednesday), "water day"; **Moku-yōbi** (Thursday) "wood day"; **Kin-yōbi** (Friday), "gold day"; **Do-yōbi** (Saturday) "soil day"; and **Nichi-yōbi** (Sunday), "sun day." Interestingly enough, our Sunday and Monday are derived from the sun and moon as well, but that's where the similarity stops.

EXPRESSIONS IN CONTEXT

 **MINI DIALOGUE 1**

A: What day is today?
   Kyō wa nan-yōbi dess ka?
   今日（きょう）は何曜日（なんようび）ですか？

B: It's Monday.
   Getsu-yōbi dess.
   月曜日（げつようび）です。

A: What day is tomorrow?
Ashita wa nan-yōbi dess ka?
明日 (あした) は何曜日 (なんようび) ですか?

B: It's Friday.
Kin-yōbi dess.
金曜日 (きんようび) です。

A: What day is the wedding ceremony?
Kekkon-shiki wa nan-yōbi dess ka?
結婚式 (けっこんしき) は何曜日 (なんようび) ですか?

B: The day after tomorrow.
Asatte dess.
明後日 (あさって) です。

A: What day is the exposition?
Hakuran-kai wa nan-yōbi dess ka?
博覧会 (はくらんかい) は何曜日 (なんようび) ですか?

B: Thursday.
Moku-yōbi dess.
木曜日 (もくようび) です。

MINI DIALOGUE 5

A: Is the picnic on Saturday?
Pikunikku wa Do-yōbi dess ka?
ピクニックは土曜日（どようび）ですか？

B: No, it's on Tuesday.
Iie, Ka-yōbi dess.
いいえ、火曜日（かようび）です。

MINI DIALOGUE 6

A: What day was (it) yesterday?
Kinō wa nan-yōbi deshita ka?
昨日（きのう）は何曜日（なんようび）でしたか？

B: It was Sunday.
Nichi-yōbi deshita.
日曜日（にちようび）でした。

MINI DIALOGUE 7

A: What day was the farewell party?
Sōbetsu-kai wa nan-yōbi deshita ka?
送別会（そうべつかい）は何曜日（なんようび）でしたか？

B: It was Monday.
Getsu-yōbi deshita.
月曜日（げつようび）でした。

 **MINI DIALOGUE 8**

A: What day did you take off from work?
Yasumi wa nan-yōbi deshita ka?
休 (やす) みは何曜日 (なんようび) でしたか？

B: I took Tuesday off.
Ka-yōbi deshita.
火曜日 (かようび) でした。

 **MINI DIALOGUE 9**

A: Was the field trip on Wednesday?
Kengaku-ryokō wa Sui-yōbi deshita ka?
見学旅行 (けんがくりょこう) は水曜日 (すいようび) でしたか？

B: No, it was on Friday.
Iie, Kin-yōbi deshita.
いいえ、金曜日 (きんようび) でした。

DAYS AND WEEKS

day before yesterday	previous day	next day
o-totoi	**mae no hi**	**tsugi no hi**
一昨日 (おととい)	前 (まえ) の日 (ひ)	次 (つぎ) の日 (ひ)

weekday
heijitsu
平日 (へいじつ)

day off from work
kyūka
休暇 (きゅうか)

next week
raishū
来週 (らいしゅう)

weekend
shūmatsu
週末 (しゅうまつ)

calendar
karendā
カレンダー

last week
senshū
先週 (せんしゅう)

national holiday
saijitsu
祭日 (さいじつ)

this week
konshū
今週 (こんしゅう)

week before last
sen-senshū
先々週 (せんせんしゅう)

EVENTS

banquet
enkai
宴会 (えんかい)

concert
konsāto
コンサート

fireworks
hanabi
花火 (はなび)

cocktail party
kakuteru-pātii
カクテルパーティー

game; match
shiai
試合 (しあい)

fireworks display
hanabi-taikai
花火大会 (はなびたい
かい)

welcome party
kangei-kai
歓迎会 (かんげいかい)

golf tournament
gorufu no konpe
ゴルフのコンペ

cherry blossom viewing
hanami/o-hanami
花見 (はなみ) ／
お花見 (はなみ)

funeral
o-sōshiki
お葬式 (そうしき)

baseball game
yakyū no shiai
野球 (やきゅう)
の試合 (しあい)

CHAPTER 7

Days, Months and Years

Remembering the names of the months is simple in Japanese. Just combine numbers (see Chapter 4) with **gatsu** (month). Thus, **Hachi-gatsu** is the eighth month, August; **Jūni-gatsu** is the twelfth month, December; and **Ichi-gatsu** is the first month, January.

WORDS & EXPRESSIONS

today
kyō
今日 (きょう)

tomorrow
ashita
明日 (あした)

the 1st
tsuitachi
1日／一日 (ついたち)

the 2nd
futsuka
2日／二日 (ふつか)

the 3rd
mikka
3日／三日 (みっか)

the 4th
yokka
4日／四日 (よっか)

the 5th
itsuka
5日／五日 (いつか)

the 6th
muika
6日／六日 (むいか)

the 7th
nanoka
7日／七日 (なのか)

what day (of the month)
nan-nichi
何日 (なんにち)

exhibition
tenran-kai
展覧会 (てんらんかい)

festival
o-matsuri
お祭 (まつ) り

this month
kongetsu
今月 (こんげつ)

next month
raigetsu
来月 (らいげつ)

January
Ichi-gatsu
1月 (いちがつ)

February	June	October
Ni-gatsu	**Roku-gatsu**	**Jū-gatsu**
2月 (にがつ)	6月 (ろくがつ)	10月 (じゅうがつ)
March	July	November
San-gatsu	**Shichi-gatsu**	**Jū-ichi-gatsu**
3月 (さんがつ)	7月 (しちがつ)	11月 (じゅういちがつ)
April	August	December
Shi-gatsu	**Hachi-gatsu**	**Jū-ni-gatsu**
4月 (しがつ)	8月 (はちがつ)	12月 (じゅうにがつ)
May	September	
Go-gatsu	**Ku-gatsu**	
5月 (ごがつ)	9月 (くがつ)	

EXAMPLES

Today is the 1st.
Kyō wa tsuitachi dess.
今日 (きょう) は1日／一日 (ついたち) です。

Tomorrow is the 2nd.
Ashita wa futsuka dess.
明日 (あした) は2日／二日 (ふつか) です。

What's the date?　　　　**What's the date of the exhibition?**
Nan-nichi dess ka?　　　**Tenran-kai wa nan-nichi dess ka?**
何日 (なんにち) ですか？　展覧会 (てんらんかい) は何日 (なんにち) ですか？

This month is January.
Kongetsu wa Ichi-gatsu dess.
今月 (こんげつ) は1月 (いちがつ) です。

Next month is February.
Raigetsu wa Ni-gatsu dess.
来月 (らいげつ) は2月 (にがつ) です。

What month is it?
Nan-gatsu dess ka?
何月 (なんがつ) ですか？

What month and what day is it?
Nan-gatsu nan-nichi dess ka?
何月 (なんがつ) 何日 (なんにち) ですか？

THE MOON AND THE MONTHS

Gatsu (month), a variant of **getsu**, as in **Getsu-yōbi** (Monday), literally means "moon". The moon, as we know, became associated with months because it circles the Earth in about 29 days. You could think of the Japanese months as the first moon, second moon, third moon, and so on.

Speaking of the moon, the Japanese have long celebrated "moon viewing". Called **tsuki-mi**, it was often a gathering of nobles and courtiers who relaxed on a veranda, gazed at the autumn moon, and composed short, poetic verses.

EXPRESSIONS IN CONTEXT

 **MINI DIALOGUE 1**

A: What's the date today?
  Kyō wa nan-nichi dess ka?
  今日 (きょう) は何日 (なんにち) ですか？

B: It's the 5th.
  Itsuka dess.
  5日 (いつか) です。

 MINI DIALOGUE 2

A: What's the date tomorrow?
   Ashita wa nan-nichi dess ka?
   明日 (あした) は何日 (なんにち) ですか？

B: It's the 6th.
   Muika dess.
   6日 (むいか) です。

 MINI DIALOGUE 3

A: What's the date of the festival?
   O-matsuri wa nan-nichi dess ka?
   お祭 (まつ) りは何日 (なんにち) ですか？

B: It's the 1st.
   Tsuitachi dess.
   1日 (ついたち) です。

MINI DIALOGUE 4

A: What month is it? (lit., What month is this month?)
   Kongetsu wa nan-gatsu dess ka?
   今月 (こんげつ) は何月 (なんがつ) ですか？

B: It's January.
   Ichi-gatsu dess.
   1月 (いちがつ) です。

MINI DIALOGUE 5

A: What month is the exhibition?
   Tenran-kai wa nan-gatsu dess ka?
   展覧会 (てんらんかい) は何月 (なんがつ) ですか？

B: It's February.
   Ni-gatsu dess.
   2月 (にがつ) です。

 **MINI DIALOGUE 6**

A: What's the date today?
Kyō wa nan-gatsu nan-nichi dess ka?
今日 (きょう) は何月 (なんがつ)
何日 (なんにち) ですか?

B: It's June 1st.
Roku-gatsu tsuitachi dess.
6月 (ろくがつ) 1日 (ついたち)
です。

 **MINI DIALOGUE 7**

A: What's the date of the exhibition?
Tenran-kai wa nan-gatsu nan-nichi dess ka?
展覧会 (てんらんかい) は何月 (なんがつ) 何日 (なんにち) ですか?

B: The 2nd of next month.
Raigetsu no futsuka dess.
来月 (らいげつ) の2日 (ふつか) です。

DAYS OF THE MONTH

the 8th	the 10th	the 12th
yōka	**tōka**	**jū-ni-nichi**
8日 (よおか)	10日 (とおか)	12日 (じゅうににち)
the 9th	the 11th	the 13th
kokonoka	**jū-ichi-nichi**	**jū-san-nichi**
9日 (ここのか)	11日 (じゅういちにち)	13日 (じゅうさんにち)

the 14th
jū-yokka
14日 (じゅうよっか)

the 20th
hatsuka
20日 (はつか)

the 26th
ni-jū-roku-nichi
26日 (にじゅうろくにち)

the 15th
jū-go-nichi
15日 (じゅうごにち)

the 21st
ni-jū-ichi-nichi
21日 (にじゅういちにち)

the 27th
ni-jū-shichi-nichi
27日 (にじゅうしちにち)

the 16th
jū-roku-nichi
16日 (じゅうろくにち)

the 22nd
ni-jū-ni-nichi
22日 (にじゅうににち)

the 28th
ni-jū-hachi-nichi
28日 (にじゅうはちにち)

the 17th
jū-shichi-nichi
17日 (じゅうしちにち)

the 23rd
ni-jū-san-nichi
23日 (にじゅうさんにち)

the 29th
ni-jū-ku-nichi
29日 (にじゅうくにち)

the 18th
jū-hachi-nichi
18日 (じゅうはちにち)

the 24th
ni-jū-yokka
24日 (にじゅうよっか)

the 30th
san-jū-nichi
30日 (さんじゅうにち)

the 19th
jū-ku-nichi
19日 (じゅうくにち)

the 25th
ni-jū-go-nichi
25日 (にじゅうごにち)

the 31st
san-jū-ichi-nichi
31日 (さんじゅういちにち)

YEARS

this year
kotoshi
今年 (ことし)

year before last
o-totoshi
一昨年 (おととし)

year after next
sarainen
再来年 (さらいねん)

last year
kyonen
去年 (きょねん)

next year
rainen
来年 (らいねん)

every year
mai-nen/mai-toshi
毎年 (まいねん／まいとし)

2017
nisen-jū-nana-nen/nisen-jū-shichi-nen
2017年（にせんじゅうななねん／
にせんじゅうしちねん）

what year
nan-nen
何年（なんねん）

EXAMPLES

What year is it? (lit., What year is this year?)
Kotoshi wa nan-nen dess ka?
今年（ことし）は何年（なんねん）ですか？

It's 2017.
Nisen-jū-nana-nen dess.
2017年（にせんじゅうななねん）
　です。

OTHERS

season **kisetsu** 季節（きせつ）	winter **fuyu** 冬（ふゆ）	every month **mai-tsuki/mai-getsu** 毎月（まいつき／まいげつ）
spring **haru** 春（はる）	every day **mai-nichi** 毎日（まいにち）	birthday **tanjō-bi** 誕生日（たんじょうび）
summer **natsu** 夏（なつ）	every night **mai-ban** 毎晩（まいばん）	anniversary **kinen-bi** 記念日（きねんび）
autumn **aki** 秋（あき）	last month **sengetsu** 先月（せんげつ）	

CHAPTER 8

Asking Directions

With one word, **sumimasen,** you can ask a stranger a question, get a store clerk's attention, and apologize for just about anything. On top of that, you can use **sumimasen** in place of **arigato** to express thanks for a kind act; for example, when someone gives you directions or offers you something to drink.

WORDS & EXPRESSIONS

Excuse me. **Sumimasen.** すみません。	station **eki** 駅 (えき)	restroom **o-tearai** お手洗 (てあらい)
taxi stand **takushii-noriba** タクシー乗 (の) り場 (ば)	far **tōi** 遠 (とお) い	near **soba** そば
where **doko** どこ	near **chikai** 近 (ちか) い	elevator **erebētā** エレベーター
over there; that place **asoko** あそこ	map **chizu** 地図 (ちず)	straight ahead **koko wo massugu** ここをまっすぐ
here; this place **koko** ここ	on the map **chizu de** 地図 (ちず) で	in front **mae** 前 (まえ)

Shinjuku (*See MAJOR CITIES/STREETS IN TOKYO)
Shinjuku
新宿 (しんじゅく)

pharmacy
kusuri-ya/yakkyoku
薬屋 (くすりや) ／薬局 (やっきょく)

EXAMPLES

Where's the nearest taxi stand?
Moyori no takushii-noriba wa doko dess ka?
最寄 (もよ) りのタクシー乗 (の) り場 (ば) はどこですか？

It's over there.
Asoko dess.
あそこです。

Where am I?/Where's this place?
Koko wa doko dess ka?
ここはどこですか？

Is the station far?
Eki wa tōi dess ka?
駅 (えき) は遠 (とお) いですか？

No, it's nearby.
Iie, chikai dess.
いいえ、近 (ちか) いです。

Where's the restroom?
O-tearai wa doko dess ka?
お手洗 (てあらい) はどこですか？

It's near the elevator.
Erebētā no soba dess.
エレベーターのそばです。

Is the pharmacy straight ahead?
Kusuri-ya/Yakkyoku wa koko wo massugu dess ka?
薬屋 (くすりや) ／薬局 (やっきょく) はここをまっすぐですか？

Yes, it's in front of the station.
Hai, eki no mae dess.
はい、駅 (えき) の前 (まえ) です。

Where on the map is Shinjuku?
Shinjuku wa chizu de doko dess ka?
新宿 (しんじゅく) は地図 (ちず) でどこですか？

MAJOR AREAS IN TOKYO

Ginza 銀座 (ぎんざ)	Shinjuku 新宿 (しんじゅく)	Akihabara 秋葉原 (あきはばら)
Nihonbashi 日本橋 (にほんばし)	Shibuya 渋谷 (しぶや)	Tsukiji 築地 (つきじ)
Marunouchi 丸の内 (まるのうち)	Harajuku 原宿 (はらじゅく)	Odaiba お台場 (おだいば)
Asakusa 浅草 (あさくさ)	Ikebukuro 池袋 (いけぶくろ)	Roppongi 六本木 (ろっぽんぎ)

SPEAKING ENGLISH IN JAPAN

What to do when your Japanese fails you? Speak in English. English-speaking people abound in Japan—the trick is knowing who and how to ask. Your best bet lies with young businesspeople, high school and college students. Many students, having spent years studying English, would love the chance to talk with you.

Still, when approached by a foreigner, some Japanese may be so surprised that their listening and speaking ability fail. Speak slowly and clearly. If that fails, try writing down what you want on paper.

EXPRESSIONS IN CONTEXT

 **MINI DIALOGUE 1**

A: Where's the restroom?
   O-tearai wa doko dess ka?
   お手洗（てあらい）はどこですか？

B: The restroom is near the elevator.
   O-tearai wa erebētā no soba dess.
   お手洗（てあらい）はエレベーター
   のそばです。

A: Where's the elevator?
   Erebētā wa doko dess ka?
   エレベーターはどこですか？

OTHER EXPRESSIONS

The pharmacy is in front of the station.
Kusuri-ya wa eki no mae dess.
薬屋（くすりや）は駅（えき）の前（まえ）です。

The taxi stand is straight ahead.
Takushii-noriba wa koko wo massugu dess.
タクシー乗（の）り場（ば）はここをまっすぐです。

 **MINI DIALOGUE 2**

A: Is Shinjuku far (from here)?
   Shinjuku wa tōi dess ka?
   新宿（しんじゅく）は遠（とお）いですか？

B: Yes, it's far (from here).
   Hai, tōi dess.
   はい、遠（とお）いです。

OTHER EXPRESSIONS

No, it's nearby.
Iie, chikai dess.
いいえ、近（ちか）いです。

 MINI DIALOGUE 3

A: Where on the map is the station?
　Eki wa kono chizu de doko dess ka?
　駅（えき）はこの地図（ちず）でどこですか？

B: Here it is.
　Koko dess.
　ここです。

 MINI DIALOGUE 4

A: Excuse me. Where am I?
　Sumimasen. Koko wa doko dess ka?
　すみません。ここはどこですか？

B: In Shinjuku.
　Shinjuku dess.
　新宿（しんじゅく）です。

 MINI DIALOGUE 5

A: Is the Shibuya station near here?
　Shibuya-eki wa chikai dess ka?
　渋谷駅（しぶやえき）は近（ちか）いですか？

B: Yes, it's over there.
　Hai, asoko dess.
　はい、あそこです。

PLACES

airport
kūkō
空港 (くうこう)

church
kyōkai
教会 (きょうかい)

bookstore
hon-ya
本屋 (ほんや)

bus stop
basu-tei
バス停 (てい)

embassy
taishi-kan
大使館 (たいしかん)

camera shop
kamera-ya
カメラ屋 (や)

Internet café/manga café
**Intanetto kafe/
manga kissa**
インターネットカフェ/
漫画喫茶 (まんがきっさ)

consulate
ryōji-kan
領事館 (りょうじかん)

bakery
pan-ya
パン屋 (や)

bank
ginkō
銀行 (ぎんこう)

gift shop
gifuto-shoppu
ギフトショップ

subway station
chika-tetsu no eki
地下鉄 (ちかてつ) の駅
(えき)

post office
yūbin-kyoku
郵便局 (ゆうびんきょく)

coffee shop
kissa-ten
喫茶店 (きっさてん)

parking lot
chūsha-jō
駐車場 (ちゅうしゃじょう)

store
mise
店 (みせ)

police station
keisatsu-sho
警察署 (けいさつしょ)

gas station
gasorin-sutando
ガソリンスタンド

department store
depāto
デパート

police box
kōban
交番 (こうばん)

WITHIN A BUILDING

escalator
esukarētā
エスカレーター

stairs
kaidan
階段 (かいだん)

floor
kai
階 (かい)

reception	basement	exit
uketsuke	**chika**	**deguchi**
受付 (うけつけ)	地下 (ちか)	出口 (でぐち)

in; inside	roof	
naka	**okujō**	
中 (なか)	屋上 (おくじょう)	

out; outside	entrance	
soto	**iriguchi**	
外 (そと)	入口 (いりぐち)	

EXAMPLES

What floor?
Nan-kai dess ka?
何階 (なんかい) ですか?

The second floor.
Ni-kai dess.
2階 (にかい) です。

DIRECTIONS

east	south	down
higashi	**minami**	**shita**
東 (ひがし)	南 (みなみ)	下 (した)

west	behind	right
nishi	**ushiro**	**migi**
西 (にし)	後 (うし) ろ	右 (みぎ)

north	up	left
kita	**ue**	**hidari**
北 (きた)	上 (うえ)	左 (ひだり)

CHAPTER 9
Taking the Train

If you don't know which train ticket to buy, ask a station employee (or a kind-looking stranger). Alternatively, buy the cheapest ticket and pay the remainder when you get off at the ticket gate or the fare adjustment office nearby. Make sure you ask which platform to use and which train to take; some express trains don't stop at every station.

WORDS & EXPRESSIONS

this **kono** この	[particle indicating direction] **e** へ	go **ikimahss** 行 (い) きます
train **densha** 電車 (でんしゃ)	to Osaka **Ōsaka e** 大阪 (おおさか) へ	doesn't go/don't go **ikimasen** 行 (い) きません
this train **kono densha** この電車 (でんしゃ)	bound for ~ **-yuki /-iki** 行 (ゆ) き／行 (い) き	which one **dore** どれ
Osaka **Ōsaka** 大阪 (おおさか)	bound for Osaka **Ōsaka-yuki/iki** 大阪 (おおさか) 行 (ゆ) き／ 行 (い) き	that one **are** あれ

ticket **kippu** 切符（きっぷ）	to Kyoto; as far as Kyoto **Kyōto made** 京都（きょうと）まで	platform **hōmu** ホーム
how much **ikura** いくら	Roppongi **Roppongi** 六本木（ろっぽんぎ）	#3 **san-ban** 3番（さんばん）
Kyoto **Kyōto** 京都（きょうと）	which **dono** どの	platform #3 **san-ban hōmu** 3番（さんばん）ホーム

EXAMPLES

Does this train go to Osaka?
Kono densha wa Ōsaka e ikimahss ka?
この電車（でんしゃ）は大阪（おおさか）へ行（い）きますか？

No, it doesn't go.
Iie, ikimasen.
いいえ、行（い）きません。

Which one is bound for Osaka?　　　　　　　　　　　**That one is.**
Ōsaka-yuki/iki wa dore dess ka?　　　　　　　　**Are dess.**
大阪（おおさか）行（ゆ）き／行（い）きはどれですか？　　あれです。

How much is the ticket?
Kippu wa ikura dess ka?
切符（きっぷ）はいくらですか？

How much is it to Kyoto?
Kyōto made ikura dess ka?
京都（きょうと）までいくらですか？

How much is it to Roppongi?
Roppongi made ikura dess ka?
六本木（ろっぽんぎ）までいくらですか？

Which platform is it?
Dono hōmu dess ka?
どのホームですか？

It's platform # 3.
San-ban hōmu dess.
3番（さんばん）ホームです。

JAPAN'S TRAINS

Japan has perhaps the best train and subway system in the world. Not only are trains safe, clean, and efficient, they traverse practically every part of Japan. The Japan Railways Group (JR), which owns eighty percent of Japan's rail system, offers a handy, economical rail pass called Japan Rail Pass. With this pass, you can ride throughout Japan on JR trains (including the bullet trains) as well as on JR buses and ferries. Ask your travel agent how to purchase the pass before you leave your home country because you cannot buy it in Japan.

EXPRESSIONS IN CONTEXT

 **MINI DIALOGUE 1**

A: Excuse me. Does this train go to Osaka?
   Sumimasen. Kono densha wa Ōsaka e ikimahss ka?
   すみません。この電車（でんしゃ）は大阪（おおさか）
   へ行（い）きますか？

B: Yes, it does.
   Hai, ikimahss.
   はい、行（い）きます。

 **MINI DIALOGUE 2**

A: Which one is bound for Kyoto?
   Kyōto-yuki/iki wa dore dess ka?
   京都 (きょうと) 行 (ゆ) き／
   行 (い) きはどれですか?

B: The one on platform #1.
   Ichi-ban hōmu no densha dess.
   1番 (いちばん) ホームの電車
   (でんしゃ) です。

OTHER EXPRESSIONS

Does that train go to Roppongi?
Ano densha wa Roppongi ni ikimasu ka?
あの電車 (でんしゃ) は六本木 (ろっぽんぎ) に行 (い) きますか?

Which platform does the train bound for Tokyo leave from?
Tōkyō-yuki/iki wa dono hōmu dess ka?
東京 (とうきょう) 行 (ゆ) き／行 (い) きはどのホームですか?

 **MINI DIALOGUE 3**

A: Excuse me. Is that one bound for Kyoto?
   Sumimasen. Kyōto-yuki/iki wa are dess ka?
   すみません。京都 (きょうと) 行 (ゆ) き／行 (い) きはあれですか?

B: No. It leaves from platform # 4.
   Iie. Yon-ban hōmu dess.
   いいえ。4番 (よんばん) ホームです。

OTHER EXPRESSIONS

No. It is bound for Osaka.
Iie. Are wa Ōsaka-yuki/iki dess.
いいえ。あれは大阪（おおさか）行（ゆ）き／行（い）きです。

 **MINI DIALOGUE 4**

A: How much is the ticket?
 Kippu wa ikura dess ka?
 切符（きっぷ）はいくらですか？

B: It's 540 yen.
 Gohyaku yonjū en dess.
 540円（ごひゃくよんじゅうえん）です。

OTHER EXPRESSIONS

How much is it to Osaka?
Ōsaka made ikura dess ka?
大阪（おおさか）までいくらですか？

How much is it to Tokyo?
Tōkyō made ikura dess ka?
東京（とうきょう）までいくらですか？

TYPES OF TRAINS

bullet train **shinkansen** 新幹線（しんかんせん）	express **kyūkō** 急行（きゅうこう）	local train **futsū** 普通（ふつう）
Limited Express **Tokkyū** 特急（とっきゅう）	rapid train **kaisoku** 快速（かいそく）	subway **chika-tetsu** 地下鉄（ちかてつ）

AT THE STATION

baggage checkroom
te-nimotsu ichiji azukari-jo
手荷物 (てにもつ) 一時 (いちじ)
預り所 (あずかりじょ)

kiosk, newspaper stand, station shop
kiosuku; eki no baiten
キヨスク; 駅 (えき) の売店 (ばいてん)

information office
annai-jo
案内所 (あんないじょ)

waiting room
machiai-shitsu
待合室 (まちあいしつ)

locker
rokkā
ロッカー

wicket; ticket gate
kaisatsu-guchi
改札口 (かいさつぐち)

ticket machine
(kippu no) jidō-hanbaiki
(切符 (きっぷ) の) 自動販売機 (じどう
はんばいき)

fare table
unchin-hyō
運賃表 (うんちんひょう)

timetable
jikoku-hyō
時刻表 (じこくひょう)

one-way (ticket)
katamichi(-kippu)
片道 (かたみち) (切符 (きっぷ))

round-trip (ticket)
ōfuku(-kippu)
往復 (おうふく) (切符 (きっぷ))

reserved-seat ticket
zaseki shitei-ken
座席指定券 (ざせきしていけん)

ON THE PLATFORM

car # ~
-gō-sha
号車 (ごうしゃ)

car # 2
ni-gō-sha
2号車 (にごうしゃ)

track # ~
~ -ban-sen
番線 (ばんせん)

non-smoking car
kin'en-sha
禁煙車 (きんえんしゃ)

non-reserved seat
jiyū-seki
自由席 (じゆうせき)

reserved seat
shitei-seki
指定席 (していせき)

dining car
shokudō-sha
食堂車 (しょくどうしゃ)

porter
akabō
赤帽 (あかぼう)

conductor
shashō
車掌 (しゃしょう)

station employee
eki-in
駅員 (えきいん)

line (train)
-sen
線 (せん)

box lunch sold at stations or on trains
eki-ben
駅弁 (えきべん)

transfer
nori-kae
乗 (の) り換 (か) え

Chuo Line (train line from Tokyo to Nagano Prefecture)
Chūō-sen
中央線 (ちゅうおうせん)

EXAMPLES

Which track number is it?
Nan-ban-sen dess ka?
何番線 (なんばんせん) ですか？

It's track # 3.
San-ban-sen dess.
３番線 (さんばんせん) です。

Which cars have non-reserved seats?
Jiyū-seki wa nan-gō-sha dess ka?
自由席 (じゆうせき) は何号車
(なんごうしゃ) ですか？

Do I transfer at Tokyo Station?
Tōkyō eki de nori-kae dess ka?
東京駅 (とうきょうえき) で乗 (の)
り換 (か) えですか？

Yes, you transfer to the Chuo Line.
Hai, Chūō-sen ni nori-kae dess.
はい、中央線 (ちゅうおうせん)
に乗 (の) り換 (か) えです。

You transfer to the subway.
Chikatetsu ni nori-kae dess.
地下鉄 (ちかてつ) に乗 (の)
り換 (か) えです。

CHAPTER 10

Taxis and Buses

If you can't find taxis on the street, you can usually get them at designated areas near train stations. Empty taxis display a red sign in *kanji*; full ones, a green sign. Try to have the address of your destination written in Japanese; this can be very helpful when riding taxis or buses.

WORDS & EXPRESSIONS

Ginza
Ginza
銀座 (ぎんざ)

to; as far as
made
まで

where
dochira
どちら

to Ginza
Ginza made
銀座 (ぎんざ) まで

please go
itte kudasai
行 (い) ってください

to the right
migi e
右 (みぎ) へ

to the left
hidari e
左 (ひだり) へ

please turn
magatte kudasai
曲 (ま) がってください

that
ano
あの

corner
kado
角 (かど)

at that corner
ano kado de
あの角 (かど) で

please stop (a car)
tomete kudasai
止 (と) めてください

trunk (of a car)
toranku
トランク

[direct object particle]
wo
を

Kanda (place name in Tokyo)
Kanda
神田 (かんだ)

stop at **ni tomarimahss** に止 (と) まります	when we get there **tsuitara** 着 (つ) いたら	please break (into change) **kuzushite kudasai** くずしてください
bus **basu** バス	please tell **oshiete kudasai** 教 (おし) えてください	
here **koko** ここ	how much **ikura** いくら	

EXAMPLES

Please go to Ginza.
Ginza made itte kudasai.
銀座 (ぎんざ) まで行 (い) ってください。

Please turn to the right.
Migi e magatte kudasai.
右 (みぎ) へ曲 (ま) がってください。

Please stop at that corner.
Ano kado de tomete kudasai.
あの角 (かど) で止 (と) めてください。

Please open the trunk.
Toranku wo akete kudasai.
トランクを開 (あ) けてください。

Does this bus stop at Kanda?
Kono basu wa Kanda ni tomarimahss ka?
このバスは神田 (かんだ) に止 (と) まりますか?

Please tell me when we get there.
Tsuitara, oshiete kudasai.
着 (つ) いたら、教 (おし) えてください。

How much is it?
Ikura dess ka?
いくらですか？

1,000-yen note
sen-en satsu
千円札 (せんえんさつ)

Please break this 1,000-yen note.
Sen-en satsu wo kuzushite kudasai.
千円札 (せんえんさつ) をくずしてください。

BUSES

In major cities, you usually pay a flat fee for riding a bus. Sometimes you pay when you get on, sometimes when you get off.

In smaller cities and rural areas, you usually pay according to the distance traveled. As you get on, look for a machine that automatically gives you a ticket with a number on it. This ticket, which indicates where you got on the bus, determines your fare. Hand over the ticket with your fare when you get off the bus. (If you get on at the terminal station, you don't get a ticket.) In some routes, the driver asks you where you get off and then tells you how much you need to pay.

EXPRESSIONS IN CONTEXT

 **MINI DIALOGUE 1**

A: **Where to?**
   Dochira made?
   どちらまで？

B: **Please go to Kanda.**
   Kanda made itte kudasai.
   神田 (かんだ) まで行 (い) ってください。

OTHER EXPRESSIONS

Please go to that corner.
Ano kado made itte kudasai.
あの角 (かど) まで行 (い) ってください。

Please turn to the left.
Hidari e magatte kudasai.
左 (ひだり) へ曲 (ま) がってください。

Excuse me. Please turn right.
Sumimasen. Migi e magatte kudasai.
すみません。右 (みぎ) へ曲 (ま) がってください。

Please stop here.   **How much is it?**
Koko de tomete kudasai.   **Ikura dess ka?**
ここで止 (と) めてください。   いくらですか？

 **MINI DIALOGUE 2**

A: **Does this bus stop at Ginza?**
   Kono basu wa Ginza ni tomarimahss ka?
   このバスは銀座 (ぎんざ) に止 (と) まりますか？

B: **Yes, it does.**
   Hai, tomarimahss.
   はい、止 (と) まります。

No. (It doesn't)	**How many stops is it?**
Iie.	**Ikutsume dess ka?**
いいえ。	いくつ目 (め) ですか?

 MINI DIALOGUE 3

A: **Excuse me. Please break this.** (give me some change for this note)
Sumimasen. Kore wo kuzushite kudasai.
すみません。これをくずしてください。

B: **Here you are.**
Hai, dōzo.
はい、どうぞ。

A: **Thank you.**
Dōmo arigatō.
どうもありがとう。

Please break this 5,000-yen note.
Go-sen-en satsu wo kuzushite kudasai.
5000円札 (ごせんえんさつ) をくずしてください。

TAXIS

Tourists should check taxi fares and if credit cards can be used, with the tourist information center in the city they're in, because it's very complicated and subject to change. Fares also vary depending on the city. In Tokyo, the rates start at 730 yen, while in Kyoto the fares start from 630 yen for a medium-sized car and 610 yen for a compact car. These are subject to change, so be sure to check the rates right before your trip to Japan. Most of the taxis should accept credit card payments, but it's always best to ask before getting into the taxi.

taxi
takushii
タクシー

intersection
kōsaten
交差点 (こうさてん)

traffic light
shingō
信号 (しんごう)

red light
aka-shingō
赤信号 (あかしんごう)

green light
ao-shingō
青信号 (あおしんごう)

Please let me out.
Oroshite kudasai.
降 (お) ろしてください。

receipt
ryōshū-sho
領収書 (りょうしゅうしょ)

BUSES

bus stop
basu-tei
バス停 (てい)

buzzer (to indicate you want to get off)
buzā
ブザー

bus # 3
san-ban no basu
3番 (さんばん) のバス

OTHERS

ship **fune** 船 (ふね)	excursion boat **yūran-sen** 遊覧船 (ゆうらんせん)	entrance to board; landing **nori-ba** 乗 (の) り場 (ば)
ferry **ferii** フェリー	ticket **kippu** 切符 (きっぷ)	

EXAMPLES

Please turn left at that intersection.
Ano kōsaten de hidari ni magatte kudasai.
あの交差点 (こうさてん) で左 (ひだり) に曲 (ま) がってください。

Please give me a receipt.
Ryōshū-sho wo kudasai.
領収書 (りょうしゅうしょ) をください。

Where's a bus stop?
Basu-tei wa doko dess ka?
バス停 (てい) はどこですか？

How much is the ticket?
Kippu wa ikura dess ka?
切符 (きっぷ) はいくらですか？

CHAPTER 11

Asking About Schedules

Need to know when something will take place? For time, say **Nan-ji dess ka?** (What time is it/will it be?) and for dates, **Nan-nichi dess ka?** (What day/date is it/will it be?) When asking a stranger a question, remember to start off with **Sumimasen.** (For information about numbers, see Chapter 4.)

WORDS & EXPRESSIONS

when **itsu** いつ	breakfast **asa-gohan** 朝 (あさ) ごはん	tomorrow **ashita** 明日 (あした)
tonight; this evening **konban** 今晩 (こんばん)	after... **...no ato (de)** …の後 (あと) (で)	hot spring **onsen** 温泉 (おんせん)
tour of a city **shinai-kankō** 市内観光 (しないかんこう)	tour of **meguri** めぐり	to a hot spring **onsen e** 温泉 (おんせん) へ
what time **nan-ji** 何時 (なんじ)	tour of Kyushu **Kyūshū-meguri** 九州 (きゅうしゅう) め ぐり	museum **hakubutsu-kan** 博物館 (はくぶつかん)

what day of the week	on Saturday	on the 10th
nan-yōbi	**Do-yōbi ni**	**tōka ni**
何曜日 (なんようび)	土曜日 (どようび) に	10日 (とおか) に

on what day of the week	at 9:00
nan-yōbi ni	**ku-ji ni**
何曜日 (なんようび) に	9時 (くじ) に

EXAMPLES

When is the Kabuki performance?
Kabuki wa itsu dess ka?
歌舞伎 (かぶき) はいつですか？

It's tonight.
Konban dess.
今晩 (こんばん) です。

What time is the city tour?
Shinai-kankō wa nan-ji dess ka?
市内観光 (しないかんこう) は何時 (なんじ) ですか？

The city tour bus will leave at 9:30.
Shinai kankō basu wa ku-ji sanju-ppun ni hassha shimahss.
市内観光 (しないかんこう) バスは9時30分 (くじさんじゅっぷん) に発車 (はっしゃ) します。

Is the Kyushu tour tomorrow?
Kyūshū-meguri wa ashita dess ka?
九州 (きゅうしゅう) めぐりは明日 (あした) ですか？

Yes, it is.
Hai. Sō dess.
はい。そうです。

When will you be going to the hot spring?
Itsu onsen e ikimahss ka?
いつ温泉 (おんせん) へ行 (い) きますか？

I'll go this week.
Konshū ikimahss.
今週 (こんしゅう) 行 (い) きます。

On what day will you be going to the museum?
Nan-yōbi ni hakubutsu-kan e ikimahss ka?
何曜日 (なんようび) に博物館 (はくぶつかん) に行 (い) きますか？

I'll go on Saturday.
Do-yōbi ni ikimahss.
土曜日 (どようび) に行 (い) きます。

I'll/We'll go at 9:00.
Ku-ji ni ikimahss.
9時 (くじ) に行 (い) きます。

I'll/We'll go on the 10th.
Tōka ni ikimahss.
10日 (とおか) に行 (い) きます。

NI, E, AND WA

Here's some advice on how to use three important particles: **ni, e,** and **wa.** Use **ni** as you would "at" or "on" in a time-related expression like "at 9:30" (**ku-ji-han ni**) or "I am going on the 10th" (**Tōka ni ikimahss**). For **e**, think of "to" when it refers to destinations, as in "I am going to Tokyo" (**Tōkyō e ikimahss**). **Wa** has no corresponding English equivalent. In general, **wa** comes after the subject of a sentence, as in **Watashi wa Amerika-jin dess** (I'm American) or **Hoteru wa ii dess** (The hotel is nice). For now, whenever you say **watashi** (I), follow it with **wa**.

EXPRESSIONS IN CONTEXT

 **MINI DIALOGUE 1**

A: Is the city tour on Monday?
Shinai-kankō wa Getsu-yōbi dess ka?
市内観光 (しないかんこう) は月曜日 (げつようび) ですか?

B: It's on Saturday.
Do-yōbi dess.
土曜日 (どようび) です。

OTHER EXPRESSIONS

When is it?	What time will it be?	On what day will you go?
Itsu dess ka?	**Nan-ji dess ka?**	**Nan-yōbi ni ikimahss ka?**
いつですか?	何時 (なんじ) ですか?	何曜日 (なんようび) に行 (い) きますか?

 **MINI DIALOGUE 2**

A: When is the Kyushu tour?
Kyūshū-meguri wa itsu dess ka?
九州 (きゅうしゅう) めぐりはいつですか?

B: It's this week.
Konshū dess.
今週 (こんしゅう) です。

OTHER EXPRESSIONS

It's on the 10th.
Tōka dess.
10日 (とおか) です。

 MINI DIALOGUE 3

A: When will you go to see the cherry blossoms?
   O-hanami niwa itsu ikimahss ka?
   お花見 (はなみ) にはいつ行 (い) きますか？

B: I'll go the day after tomorrow.
   Asatte ikimahss.
   明後日 (あさって) 行 (い) きます。

OTHER EXPRESSIONS

Will you go tonight?
Konban ikimahss ka?
今晩 (こんばん) 行 (い) きますか？

 MINI DIALOGUE 4

A: When will you go to the museum?
   Itsu hakubutsu-kan e ikimahss ka?
   いつ博物館 (はくぶつかん) へ行 (い) きますか？

B: I'll go after breakfast.
   Asa-gohan no ato de ikimahss.
   朝 (あさ) ごはんの後 (あと) で行 (い) きます。

OTHER EXPRESSIONS

After breakfast.
Asa-gohan no ato dess.
朝 (あさ) ごはんの後 (あと) です。

I'll go at 10:00.
Jū-ji ni ikimahss.
10時 (じゅうじ) に行 (い) きます。

SCHEDULING SOMETHING

meal
shokuji
食事 (しょくじ)

tomorrow morning
ashita no asa
明日 (あした) の朝 (あさ)

traveler/tourist
ryokō-sha
旅行者 (りょこうしゃ)

before
no mae (ni)
の前 (まえ) (に)

every week
mai-shū
毎週 (まいしゅう)

travel bureau
ryokō-sentā
旅行 (りょこう) センター

before a meal
shokuji no mae
食事 (しょくじ) の前 (まえ)

next week
raishū
来週 (らいしゅう)

group tour
dantai-ryokō
団体旅行 (だんたいりょこう)

right away
sugu
すぐ

last week
senshū
先週 (せんしゅう)

overseas travel
kaigai-ryokō
海外旅行 (かいがいりょこう)

soon; shortly
mō sugu
もうすぐ

summer vacation
natsu-yasumi
夏休 (なつやす) み

travel insurance
ryokō-hoken
旅行保険 (りょこうほけん)

one of these days
chikai uchi ni
近 (ちか) いうちに

winter vacation
fuyu-yasumi
冬休 (ふゆやす) み

guidebook
gaido-bukku
ガイドブック

alone/by onself
hitori de
一人 (ひとり) で

EXAMPLES

I'll go one of these days.
Chikai uchi ni ikimahss.
近 (ちか) いうちに行 (い) きます。

I'll go with a group tour.
Dantai-ryokō de ikimahss.
団体旅行 (だんたいりょこう) で行 (い) きます。

I'll go by myself.
Hitori de ikimahss.
一人 (ひとり) で行 (い) きます。

CHAPTER 12

Talking About Food

If you plan to have a meal with Japanese people, you should master two phrases: **itadakimahss** and **gochisō-sama deshita**. Say **itadakimahss** before you start eating and **gochisō-sama deshita** when you have finished. All Japanese say these phrases at meals, and you'll leave a good impression if you do too.

WORDS & EXPRESSIONS

green tea **o-cha** お茶 (ちゃ)	this **kore** これ	taste **aji** 味 (あじ)
[direct object particle] **o** お	what **nani/nan** 何 (なに／なん)	how **dō-yatte** どうやって
please (do something) **dōzo** どうぞ	**o-manjū** (bun with bean- jam filling) おまんじゅう	with what **nani/nan de** 何 (なに／なん) で
sweets **o-kashi** お菓子 (かし)	inside **naka** 中 (なか)	sweet **amai** 甘 (あま) い
how about **ikaga** いかが	what kind of **don-na** どんな	delicious **oishii** おいしい

Isn't it?	[subject particle]	cookie
Ne.	**ga**	**kukkii**
ね。	が	クッキー

more; some more	hungry
motto	**suite imahss**
もっと	空 (す) いています

stomach	full
o-naka	**ippai**
お腹 (なか)	一杯 (いっぱい)

EXAMPLES

Please have some tea.
O-cha wo dōzo.
お茶 (ちゃ) をどうぞ。

Thank you. (I'll have some.)
Itadakimahss.
いただきます。

No, thank you.
Kekkō dess.
けっこうです。

How about some sweets?
O-kashi wa ikaga dess ka?
お菓子 (かし) はいかがですか?

What's this?
Kore wa nan dess ka?
これは何 (なん) ですか?

It's a manjū.
O-manjū dess.
おまんじゅうです。

What's inside?
Naka wa nan dess ka?
中 (なか) は何 (なん) ですか?

What does it taste like?
Don-na aji dess ka?
どんな味 (あじ) ですか?

How do you eat this?
Kore wa dō-yatte tabemahss ka?
これはどうやって食 (た) べますか？

What do you eat this with?
Kore wa nan de tabemahss ka?
これは何 (なん) で食べますか？

It's delicious, isn't it?
Oishii dess ne.
おいしいですね。

Thank you. (It was delicious.)
Gochisō-sama deshita.
ごちそうさまでした。

How about some more?
Motto ikaga dess ka?
もっといかがですか？

I'm hungry.
O-naka ga suite imahss.
お腹 (なか) が空 (す) いています。

I'm full.
O-naka ga ippai dess.
お腹 (なか) が一杯 (いっぱい) です。

LOANWORDS

Thousands of words in Japanese are loanwords, words derived from other languages. Try guessing the meanings of these drinks: **Koka-kōra, kōhii,** and **biiru.** Did you guess Coca-Cola, coffee, and beer? With exposure, you can easily increase your vocabulary just by learning loanwords.

Be careful, though, because not all loanwords come from English. For instance, **pan** (bread) comes from Portuguese, **ikura** (salmon roe) from Russian, and **arubaito** (part-time job) from German.

EXPRESSIONS IN CONTEXT

 MINI DIALOGUE 1

A: **Please have some sweets.**
   O-kashi wo dōzo.
   お菓子 (かし) をどうぞ。

B: **Thank you.**
   Hai, itadakimahss.
   はい、いただきます。

OTHER EXPRESSIONS

No, thank you.
Iie, kekkō dess.
いいえ、けっこうです。

 MINI DIALOGUE 2

A: **What's this?**
   Kore wa nan dess ka?
   これは何 (なん) ですか?

B: **It's a manjū.**
   O-manjū dess.
   おまんじゅうです。

A: **What does it taste like?**
   Don-na aji dess ka?
   どんな味 (あじ) ですか?

B: **It's sweet.**
   Amai dess.
   甘 (あま) いです。

OTHER EXPRESSIONS

What's inside?
Naka wa nan dess ka?
中 (なか) は何 (なん) ですか?

 **MINI DIALOGUE 3**

A: How about a manjū?
O-manjū wa ikaga dess ka?
おまんじゅうはいかがですか？

B: Thank you.
Hai, itadakimahss.
はい、いただきます。

A: Delicious, isn't it?
Oishii dess ne.
おいしいですね。

B: How about some more?
Motto ikaga dess ka?
もっといかがですか？

A: No, thank you. Thank you. (It was wonderful.)
Iie, kekkō dess. Gochisō-sama deshita.
いいえ、けっこうです。ごちそうさまでした。

OTHER EXPRESSIONS

Sweet, isn't it?
Amai dess ne.
甘 (あま) いですね。

The sweets are delicious, aren't they?
O-kashi wa oishii dess ne.
お菓子 (かし) はおいしいですね。

I'm full.
O-naka ga ippai dess.
お腹 (なか) が一杯 (いっぱい) です。

MINI DIALOGUE 4

A: I'm hungry.
   O-naka ga suite imahss.
   お腹 (なか) が空 (す) いています。

B: Please have some cookies.
   Kukkii wo dōzo.
   クッキーをどうぞ。

A: Thank you. (I'll have some.)
   Itadakimahss.
   いただきます。

DESCRIBING FOOD

raw **nama** 生 (なま)	hard; tough **katai** 固 (かた) い	spicy **karai** 辛 (から) い
not tasty **oishiku nai** おいしくない	soft; tender **yawarakai** 柔 (やわ) らかい	salty **shoppai** 塩 (しょ) っぱい
new; fresh **atarashii** 新 (あたら) しい	hot **atsui** 熱 (あつ) い	sour **suppai** 酸 (す) っぱい
old; stale **furui** 古 (ふる) い	cold (to the touch) **tsumetai** 冷 (つめ) たい	bitter **nigai** 苦 (にが) い

DRINKS

water
mizu
水 (みず)

coffee
kōhii
コーヒー

black tea
kōcha
紅茶 (こうちゃ)

Coca-Cola
Koka-kōra
コカコーラ

beer
biiru
ビール

wine
wain
ワイン

shochu (distilled spirit
usually drunk with water
or a mixer)
shōchū
焼酎 (しょうちゅう)

whisky
uisukii
ウイスキー

whisky and water
uisukii no mizu-wari
ウイスキーの水割 (みず
わ) り

FRUIT

fruit
kudamono;
furūtsu
果物 (くだもの); フ
ルーツ)

apple
ringo
りんご

pear
nashi
梨 (なし)

peach
momo
桃 (もも)

grape
budō
ぶどう

tangerine
mikan
みかん

orange
orenji
オレンジ

watermelon
suika
すいか

melon
meron
メロン

persimmon
kaki
柿 (かき)

VEGETABLES

vegetable
yasai
野菜 (やさい)

potato
jagaimo
じゃがいも

carrot
ninjin
にんじん

lettuce
retasu
レタス

cucumber
kyūri
きゅうり

shiitake (type of mushroom)
shiitake
しいたけ

cabbage
kyabetsu
キャベツ

corn
tōmorokoshi
とうもろこし

lotus root
renkon
レンコン

pumpkin
kabocha
かぼちゃ

onion
tamanegi
玉 (たま) ねぎ

bamboo shoot
takenoko
竹 (たけ) の子 (こ)

tomato
tomato
トマト

eggplant
nasu
なす

salad
sarada
サラダ

MEAT, SEAFOOD, POULTRY, DAIRY PRODUCTS

meat
niku
肉 (にく)

pork
buta-niku
豚肉 (ぶたにく)

egg
tamago
玉子 (たまご)

beef
gyū-niku
牛肉 (ぎゅうにく)

chicken
tori-niku
鶏肉 (とりにく)

fish
sakana
魚 (さかな)

shrimp
ebi
エビ

octopus
tako
タコ

yogurt
yōguruto
ヨーグルト

cuttlefish
ika
イカ

milk
gyū-nyū
牛乳 (ぎゅうにゅう)

ice cream
aisu-kuriimu
アイスクリーム

OTHERS

cooked rice (can also mean "meal")
gohan
ごはん

tofu
tōfu
豆腐 (とうふ)

miso (bean paste)
miso
味噌 (みそ)

seaweed
nori
海苔 (のり)

chopsticks
o-hashi
お箸 (はし)

cake
kēki
ケーキ

rice cracker
senbei
せんべい

CHAPTER 13

Dining Out

Travelers should try to eat at restaurants where the local residents are the main patrons. (Your hotel should know a good one nearby, or search online.) If you don't know what to order, try a set meal called a **teishoku**. Ask **Teishoku wa arimahss ka?** (Do you have set meals?) to find out if the restaurant serves them or not.

WORDS & EXPRESSIONS

this **kono** この	[subject particle] **ga** が	don't have **arimasen** ありません
vicinity **hen** へん	there is; there are **arimahss** あります	what **nani** 何 (なに)
in this vicinity; around here **kono hen ni** このへんに	tempura (deep-fried food) **tenpura** 天 (てん) ぷら	drink **o-nomimono** お飲物 (のみもの)
restaurant **resutoran** レストラン	[subject particle, frequently used when distinguishing one from another] **wa** は	beer **biiru** ビール

saké (Japanese rice wine)
o-sake
お酒 (さけ)

please (lit., I make a request)
o-negai shimahss
お願 (ねが) いします

sushi (vinegared rice and raw fish)
o-sushi
お寿司 (すし)

please give
kudasai
ください

Excuse me.
Sumimasen.
すみません。

water
mizu
水 (みず)

curry with rice
karē-raisu
カレーライス

EXAMPLES

Is there a restaurant around here?
Kono hen ni resutoran wa arimahss ka?
このへんにレストランはありますか？

We don't have tempura.
Tenpura wa arimasen.
天 (てん) ぷらはありません。

What do you have?
Nani ga arimahss ka?
何 (なに) がありますか？

How about a drink?
O-nomimono wa?
お飲物 (のみもの) は？

Beer, please.
Biiru wo o-negai shimahss.
ビールをお願 (ねが) いします。

Sushi, please.
O-sushi wo kudasai.
お寿司 (すし) をください。

Excuse me. May I have some water?
Sumimasen. Mizu wo kudasai.
すみません。水 (みず) をください。

Curry with rice, please.
Karē-raisu wo kudasai.
カレーライスをください。

Certainly, sir/ma'am.
Kashikomarimashita.
かしこまりました。

EATING IN JAPANESE RESTAURANTS

Eating in Japan is a great experience. The food is good, healthy, and there's a great variety to choose from. But what if you can't read the menu? There's no need to worry, because many places have plastic food displays. Just take the waiter to the display case, and point to what you want to eat.

One tip for sushi lovers: If you don't know how to order sushi, call out **Nigiri-zushi, ichinin-mae!** and you'll get a tray of various types of sushi. You can also point, this time to the real thing in the showcase at the counter, to other delicacies you want to try. If you want to specify that you don't eat a certain item, such as pork, puffer fish or sea urchin, you can say **Butaniku/Fugu/Uni wa tabarera-masen** to mean "I don't eat pork/puffer fish/sea urchin."

EXPRESSIONS IN CONTEXT

 **MINI DIALOGUE 1**

A: Is there a restaurant around here?
   Kono hen ni resutoran wa arimahss ka?
   このへんにレストランはありますか？

B: Yes, there is.
   Hai, arimahss.
   はい、あります。

MINI DIALOGUE 2

A: Do you have tempura?
Tenpura wa arimahss ka?
天 (てん) ぷらはありますか?

B: Yes, we have.
Hai, arimahss.
はい、あります。

MINI DIALOGUE 3

A: Tempura, please.
Tenpura wo o-negai shimahss.
天 (てん) ぷらをお願 (ねが) いします。

B: Certainly, sir.
Kashikomarimashita.
かしこまりました。

MINI DIALOGUE 4

A: Do you have curry with rice?
Karē-raisu wa arimahss ka?
カレーライスはありますか?

B: No, we don't have curry with rice.
Iie, karē-raisu wa arimasen.
いいえ、カレーライスはありません。

MINI DIALOGUE 5

A: Do you have sushi?
O-sushi wa arimahss ka?
お寿司 (すし) はありますか?

B: No, we don't have sushi.
Iie, o-sushi wa arimasen.
いいえ、お寿司 (すし) はありません。

A: What do you have?
Nani ga arimahss ka?
何 (なに) がありますか?

B: We have curry with rice.
Karē raisu ga arimahss.
カレーライスがあります。

 **MINI DIALOGUE 6**

A: How about a drink?
　 O-nomimono wa?
　 お飲物 (のみもの) は？

B: Saké, please.
　 O-sake wo kudasai.
　 お酒 (さけ) をください。

OTHER EXPRESSIONS

Water, please.
Mizu wo o-negai shimahss.
水 (みず) をお願 (ねが) いします。

Excuse me. Beer, please.
Sumimasen. Biiru wo kudasai.
すみません。ビールをください。

MENU ITEMS

Japanese cuisine
Nihon-ryōri
日本料理 (にほんりょうり)

Chinese cuisine
**Chūgoku-ryōri/
Chūka-ryōri**
中国料理 (ちゅうごくりょうり)／中華料理 (ちゅうかりょうり)

set meal (includes main dish, soup, pickles, and rice)
teishoku
定食 (ていしょく)

soup
o-sui-mono
お吸 (す) い物 (もの)

pickle
tsuke-mono
漬 (つ) け物 (もの)

popular dish of meat, vegetable, bean curd, etc.
suki-yaki
すき焼 (や) き

grilled, skewered chicken
yakitori
焼 (や) き鳥 (とり)

pork cutlet
tonkatsu
とんかつ

broiled eel and rice
una-don
うな丼 (どん)

noodles (white and fat)
udon
うどん

buckwheat noodles (dark and thin)
soba
そば

SUSHI TOPPINGS

tuna **maguro** まぐろ	mackerel **saba** さば	shrimp **ebi** えび	sea urchin **uni** うに
bonito **katsuo** かつお	horse mackerel **iwashi** いわし	octopus **tako** たこ	
yellowtail **hamachi** はまち	salmon **sake** さけ	squid **ika** いか	
sardine **iwashi** いわし	flatfish **hirame** ひらめ	salmon roe **ikura** イクラ	

TABLEWARE

rice bowl **chawan** 茶碗 (ちゃわん)	saké cup **sakazuki** 杯 (さかずき)	hot or cold hand towel used to wipe one's hands before eating **o-shibori** おしぼり
teacup **yu-nomi** 湯 (ゆ) のみ	plate **sara** 皿 (さら)	
cup; glass **koppu** コップ	chopsticks **o-hashi** お箸 (はし)	spoon **supūn** スプーン
saké bottle **tokkuri** 徳利 (とっくり)	fork **fōku** フォーク	napkin **napukin** ナプキン

OTHERS

check (bill)	credit card
o-kanjō	**kurejitto-kādo**
お勘定（かんじょう）	クレジットカード

EXAMPLES

May I please have the check?
O-kanjō wo o-negai shimahss.
お勘定（かんじょう）をお願（ねが）いします。

We'd like to pay separately.
Betsu-betsu ni o-negai shimahss.
別々（べつべつ）にお願（ねが）いします。

It's my treat.
Watashi no ogori dess.
私（わたし）のおごりです。

How much is it?
Ikura dess ka?
いくらですか？

May I pay with a credit card?
Kurejitto-kādo de haraemahss ka?
クレジットカードで払（はら）えますか？

It's delicious.
Oishii dess.
おいしいです。

It was delicious.
Oishikatta dess.
おいしかったです。

CHAPTER 14

Making a Phone Call

To use a public phone, put in coins (usually a 10 yen or 100 yen coin), or a telephone card, wait for a dial tone and dial the number. The costs vary, about 10 yen per minute for calls within your area code, and less outside the area. Calls to cell phones are usually more expensive. Public phones are now harder to find in the street, so try hotels, stations, or airports. Alternatively, you could rent a local phone from service providers like SoftBank and Rentaphone and have it delivered to your first night's accommodation. Data SIM cards and pocket Wi-Fi routers are also available.

WORDS & EXPRESSIONS

Hello. (on the telephone) **Moshi-moshi.** もしもし。	please wait **o-machi kudasai** お待 (ま) ちください	isn't in; aren't in **imasen** いません
please **o-negai shimahss** お願 (ねが) いします	Sorry, but... **Sumimasen ga...** すみませんが…	who **dochira-sama** どちら様 (さま)
a moment; awhile **shibaraku** しばらく	now **ima** 今 (いま)	well **yoku** よく

can't hear **kikoemasen** 聞 (き) こえません	English language **Ei-go** 英語 (えいご)	telephone **o-denwa** お電話 (でんわ)
once more **mō ichido** もう一度 (いちど)	in English **Ei-go de** 英語 (えいご) で	make a telephone call **o-denwa shimahss** お電話 (でんわ) します
please say **itte kudasai** 言 (い) ってください	again **mata** また	Goodbye. **Sayōnara.** さようなら。

EXAMPLES

Mr. Yamada, please. (May I speak with Mr. Yamada?)
Yamada-san wo o-negai shimahss.
山田 (やまだ) さんをお願 (ねが) いします。

Please wait a moment.
Shibaraku o-machi kudasai.
しばらくお待 (ま) ちください。

Hello./Good afternoon.
Konnichiwa.
こんにちは。

How are you?
O-genki dess ka?
お元気 (げんき) ですか？

Sorry, but Mr. Yamada isn't in now.
Sumimasen ga, Yamada wa ima imasen.
すみませんが、山田 (やまだ) は今 (いま) いません。

Who is calling, please?
Dochira-sama dess ka?
どちら様（さま）ですか？

What's your name?
O-namae wa?
お名前（なまえ）は？

I can't hear you well.
Yoku kikoemasen.
よく聞（き）こえません。

Please say it once more.
Mō ichido itte kudasai.
もう一度（いちど）言（い）ってください。

Please say it in English.
Ei-go de itte kudasai.
英語（えいご）で言（い）ってください。

I'll call again.
Mata o-denwa shimahss.
またお電話（でんわ）します。

TELEPHONES

Pay phones are still used in Japan. There are four types: gray, green, blue and pink. Gray and green phones allow international calls, and you can pay by coin or calling card. You can also connect your laptop to the Internet with the gray phones. Blue phones can be used for international calls, and you can pay with credit cards. Pink phones are the rarest and only coins can be used. If you're using coins, be sure to check what's the smallest amount you can pay with—you won't get change back.

For helpful telephone services in English, refer to USEFUL TELEPHONE NUMBERS in Chapter 22, Pg 204.

EXPRESSIONS IN CONTEXT

 **MINI DIALOGUE 1**

A: Hello. May I speak to Ms. Yamada?
Moshi-moshi. Yamada-san wo o-negai shimahss.
もしもし。山田 (やまだ) さんをお願 (ねが) いします。

B: Yes. Please wait a moment.
Hai. Shibaraku o-machi kudasai.
はい。しばらくお待 (ま) ちください。

C: Hello. Yamada speaking.
Moshi-moshi. Yamada dess.
もしもし。山田 (やまだ) です。

A: Hello, Ms. Yamada. This is Brown speaking.
Konnichiwa, Yamada-san. Buraun dess.
こんにちは、山田 (やまだ) さん。ブラウンです。

C: Hello, Ms. Brown. How are you?
Konnichiwa, Buraun-san. O-genki dess ka?
こんにちは、ブラウンさん。お元気 (げんき) ですか?

A: Yes, I'm fine, thank you.
Hai, arigatō. Genki dess.
はい、ありがとう。元気 (げんき) です。

 **MINI DIALOGUE 2**

A: Hello. Is Mr. Yamada in?
   Moshi-moshi. Yamada-san wa imahss ka?
   もしもし。山田 (やまだ) さんはいますか？

B: Sorry, but he isn't in now.
   Sumimasen ga, Yamada wa ima imasen.
   すみませんが、山田 (やまだ) は今 (いま) いません。

   Who is calling, please?
   Dochira-sama dess ka?
   どちら様 (さま) ですか？

A: This is Brown. I'll call again.
   Buraun dess. Mata o-denwa shimahss.
   ブラウンです。またお電話 (でんわ) します。

B: Yes, please do.
   Hai, o-negai shimahss.
   はい、お願 (ねが) いします。

A: Goodbye.
   Sayōnara.
   さようなら。

OTHER EXPRESSIONS

Excuse me, but I can't hear you well.
Sumimasen ga, yoku kikoemasen.
すみませんが、よく聞 (き) こえません。

Please say it once more in English.
Ei-go de mō ichido itte kudasai.
英語 (えいご) でもう一度 (いちど) 言 (い) ってください。

ADDITIONAL WORDS & EXPRESSIONS

telephone number
denwa-bangō
電話番号 (でんわばんごう)

telephone directory
denwa-chō
電話帳 (でんわちょう)

cell phone
keitai-denwa
携帯電話 (けいたいでんわ)

telephone bill
denwa-ryōkin
電話料金 (でんわりょうきん)

public telephone
kōshū-denwa
公衆電話 (こうしゅうでんわ)

local telephone call
shinai-denwa
市内電話 (しないでんわ)

long distance telephone call
chōkyori-denwa
長距離電話 (ちょうきょりでんわ)

international telephone call
kokusai-denwa
国際電話 (こくさいでんわ)

operator
kōkan-shu
交換手 (こうかんしゅ)

credit card
kurejitto-kādo
クレジットカード

telephone card
terefon-kādo
テレフォンカード

extension
naisen
内線 (ないせん)

message
messēji
メッセージ

wrong number
bangō-chigai
番号 (ばんごう) 違 (ちが) い

EXAMPLES

May I leave a message?
Messēji wo o-negai dekimahss ka?
メッセージをお願 (ねが) いできますか？

You have the wrong number.
Bangō ga chigaimahss.
番号 (ばんごう) が違 (ちが) います。

May I use this phone?
O-denwa wo karite mo ii dess ka?
お電話 (でんわ) を借 (か) りてもいいですか？

Thank you for calling.
O-denwa, dōmo arigatō.
お電話 (でんわ) 、どうもありがとう。

Where's a phone?
Denwa wa doko ni arimahss ka?
電話 (でんわ) はどこにありますか？

I can't connect to the Internet. **Intānetto ni tsunagarimasen.** インターネットに つながりません。

Try one of those convenience stores. **Konbini ni itte mite kudasai.** コンビニに行 (い) ってみてください。

You can connect to the Internet at that fast food restaurant. **Ano fāsuto fūdoten de tsunagarimahss.** あのファーストフード店 (てん) でつながります。

Thank you. **Arigatō.** ありがとう。

CHAPTER 15

Using the Internet

Most computer and social media terms in Japanese are based on the English terms—such as **nettowāku** for "network", **Feisubukku** for "Facebook", **Insutaguramu** for "Instagram", and **pasuwādo** for "password", except that the intonations are almost always flat and all the consonants are followed by vowels. For example, you wouldn't make yourself understood if you said Internet instead of **Intānetto**. You can always bring a pocket WIFI router from your home country, or rent one to be delivered to your accommodation in Japan; otherwise pick up a free Wi-Fi card from airports or tourist information centers and use them in cafés, convenience stores fast-food restaurants and shopping centres to name a few.

WORDS & EXPRESSIONS

here **koko de** ここで	personal computer **pasokon** パソコン	can be used **tsukaemahss** 使 (つか) えます
the Internet **Intānetto** インターネット	lobby **robii** ロビー	here **koko wa** ここは
Can I use...? **Tsukaemahss ka?** 使 (つか) えますか?	for free **muryō de** 無料 (むりょう) で	can connect to... **tsunagarimahss** つながります

Can I connect to...?
Tsunagarimahss ka?
つながりますか?

can't connect
tsunagarimasen
つながりません

where
doko e
どこへ

Should I go?
Ikeba ii dess ka?
行 (い) けばいいですか?

in your room
o-heya de
お部屋 (へや) で

connection
setsuzoku
接続 (せつぞく)

service
sābiss
サービス

You can use...
riyō dekimahss
利用 (りよう) できます

spot
supotto
スポット

that
ano
あの

convenience store
konbini
コンビニ

Internet/cyber café
Intānetto kafe
インターネットカフェ

manga/comic café
manga kissa
漫画喫茶 (まんがきっさ)

train station
eki
駅 (えき)

fast food restaurant
fasuto fūdo ten
ファストフード店 (てん)

try
itte mite
行 (い) ってみて

platform
puratto hōmu
プラットホーム

in the middle of
chūō ni
中央 (ちゅうおう) に

at the end of
haji ni
端 (はじ) に

There is...
arimahss
あります

SIM card
shimu kādo
SIM (シム) カード

3G data SIM card
san gigadēta shimu kādo
3 (さん) ギガデータ
SIM (シム) カード

prepaid cell phone
puri peido keitai
プリペイド携帯 (けいたい)

pocket Wi-Fi router
poketto waifai
ポケットWi-Fi (ワイファイ)

Can I buy...?
... wo kaemahss ka?
…を買 (か) えますか?

Can I rent...?
... wo kariraremahss ka?
…を借 (か) りられますか?

Can I use the Internet here?
Koko de Intānetto wa tsukaemahss ka?
ここでインターネットは使 (つか) えますか?

Where should I go?
Doko e ikeba ii dess ka?
どこへ行 (い) けばいいですか?

Can I connect to the Internet here?
Koko wa Intānetto ga tsunagarimahss ka?
ここはインターネットがつながりますか?

I can't connect to the Internet.
Intānetto ni tsunagarimasen.
インターネットにつながりません。

There is no charge for using the personal computers in the lobby.
Robii no pasokon wa muryō de tsukaemahss.
ロビーのパソコンは無料 (むりょう) で使 (つか) えます。

You can use our free Wi-Fi connection service in your room.
O-heya de muryō no waifai setsuzoku sābiss wo riyō dekimahss.
お部屋 (へや) で無料 (むりょう) のWi-Fi (ワイファイ) 接続 (せつぞく) サービス
を利用 (りよう) できます。

Where is a free Wi-Fi spot?
Muryō no waifai supotto wa doko ni arimahss ka?
無料 (むりょう) のWi-Fi (ワイファイ) スポットはどこにありますか?

Try one of those convenience stores.
Konbini ni itte mite kudasai.
コンビニに行 (い) ってみてください。

There is one in the middle of the platform.
Puratto hōmu no chūō ni arimahss.
プラットホームの中央 (ちゅうおう) にあります。

Where can I buy a SIM card?
SIM kādo wa doko de kaemahss ka?
SIM (シム) カードはどこで買 (か) えますか?

FINDING FREE WI-FI SERVICE

Connecting to the Internet in Japan is fairly easy, especially if you have a pocket WiFi (you can rent one from your home country, or from the airport in Japan—most of the staff there can speak English, so don't worry if you can't speak Japanese that well). Otherwise, there are several free WiFi networks you can tap on, available at major railway stations, international airports, as well as some coffee, fast food and convenience store chains like Starbucks and Denny's.

You can also download the Japan Connected-free Wi-Fi, Free Wi-Fi Passport or Travel Japan Wi-Fi mobile apps which will give you access to 150,000 to 400,000 hot spots across the country after registration.

 **MINI DIALOGUE 1**

A: **Can I use the Internet here?**
   Koko de Intānetto wa tsukaemahss ka?
   ここでインターネットは使 (つか) えますか?

B: **Yes. You can use the Internet on the personal computers in the lobby.**
   Hai. Robii no pasokon de Intānetto ni tsunagarimahss.
   はい。ロビーのパソコンでインターネットにつながります。

MINI DIALOGUE 2

A: Can I buy a pre-paid cell phone?
Puri peido keitai wa doko de kaemahss ka?
プリペイド携帯 (けいたい) はどこで買 (か) えますか?

B: You can buy one here.
Koko de kaemahss.
ここで買 (か) えます。

OTHER EXPRESSIONS

You can buy one at a convenience store.
Konbini de kaemahss.
コンビニで買えます。

MINI DIALOGUE 3

A: I can't connect to the Internet.
Intānetto ni tsunagarimasen.
インターネットにつながりません。

B: Try one of the train stations.
Eki ni itte mite kudasai.
駅 (えき) に行 (い) ってみてください。

OTHER EXPRESSIONS

You can connect to the Internet at that fast food restaurant.
Ano fasuto fūdo ten de tsunagarimahss.
あのファストフード店 (てん) でつながります。

CHAPTER 16
Making a Reservation

Since making reservations on the phone in Japanese can be very difficult for foreigners, it's best to ask an English-speaking Japanese person in your hotel to make a reservation for you. Many websites have English translations though, so you can reserve online in advance. Sometimes, making reservations in person, can be easier than booking on the phone or online.

WORDS & EXPRESSIONS

tour bus
kankō-basu
観光 (かんこう) バス

reservation
yoyaku
予約 (よやく)

please
o-negai shimahss
お願 (ねが) いします

when
itsu
いつ

today
kyō
今日 (きょう)

tomorrow
ashita
明日 (あした)

full; no vacancy
manseki
満席 (まんせき)

the day after tomorrow
asatte
明後日 (あさって)

how about
dō
どう

all right
daijōbu
大丈夫 (だいじょうぶ)

well then
dewa
では

how many people
nan-mei-sama
何名様 (なんめいさま)

| polite equivalent to -san
-sama
様 (さま) | two people
futari
2人 (ふたり) | how much
ikura
いくら |
| one person
hitori
1人 (ひとり) | ticket
kippu
切符 (きっぷ) | name
namae
名前 (なまえ) |

EXAMPLES

I'd like to make a reservation for the tour bus to Niigata.
Niigata iki no kankō-basu no yoyaku wo o-negai shimahss.
新潟 (にいがた) 行 (い) きの観光 (かんこう) バスの予約 (よやく) をお願 (ねが) いします。

For when?
Itsu no bun dess ka?
いつの分 (ぶん) ですか?

For tomorrow.
Ashita dess.
明日 (あした) です。

Sorry, but we're full tomorrow.
Sumimasen ga, ashita wa manseki dess.
すみませんが、明日 (あした) は満席 (まんせき) です。

How about the day after tomorrow?
Asatte wa dō dess ka?
明後日 (あさって) はどうですか?

The day after tomorrow is all right.
Asatte wa daijōbu dess.
明後日 (あさって) は大丈夫 (だいじょうぶ) です。

Well then, please make the reservation for the day after tomorrow.
Dewa, asatte no yoyaku wo o-negai shimahss.
では、明後日 (あさって) の予約 (よやく) をお願 (ねが) いします。

How many people?
Nan-mei-sama dess ka?
何名様 (なんめいさま) ですか？

There are two people.
Futari dess.
2人 (ふたり) です。

How much is the ticket?
Kippu wa ikura dess ka?
切符 (きっぷ) はいくらですか？

It's 3,500 yen.
San-zen go-hyaku-en dess.
3,500円 (さんぜんごひゃくえん) です。

What's your name?
O-namae wa?
お名前 (なまえ) は？

It's Smith.
Sumisu dess.
スミスです。

UNIQUE ACCOMMODATIONS

If you want to experience lodging Japanese style, stay at a Japanese inn (**ryokan**). You'll be served a complete Japanese dinner and breakfast, and you'll sleep on bedding laid out on **tatami** (straw mat) floors. Or, try a **minshuku**, a family-run guesthouse offering lodging at a reasonable price.

For a unique experience, spend a night at a temple. Besides being able to sample the delicious and healthy temple cooking, you'll get a feel of the serenity and simplicity of temple living. Ask your travel agent or the Japan Travel Bureau for more information. Younger travelers might wish to try the capsule hotel—economical but basic, although some have included spa and hot spring facilities recently.

EXPRESSIONS IN CONTEXT

 **MINI DIALOGUE 1**

A: I'm looking to book a room for tonight.
   Konya tomaru heya wo sagashite iru no dess ga.
   今夜 (こんや) 泊 (と) まる部屋 (へや) を探 (さが) しているのですが。

B: For how many people?
   Nan-mei-sama dess ka?
   何名様 (なんめいさま) ですか?

A: Two.
   Futari dess.
   2人 (ふたり) です。

OTHER EXPRESSIONS

For the day after tomorrow.
Asatte dess.
明後日 (あさって) です。

 **MINI DIALOGUE 2**

A: How many people are there?
   Nan-mei-sama dess ka?
   何名様 (なんめいさま) ですか?

B: One person.
   Hitori dess.
   1人 (ひとり) です。

A: What's your name?
O-namae wa?
お名前 (なまえ) は？

B: My name is Smith.
Sumisu dess.
スミスです。

MINI DIALOGUE 3

A: How much is the ticket?
Kippu wa ikura dess ka?
切符 (きっぷ) はいくらですか？

B: It's 3,000 yen.
San-zen-en dess.
3,000円 (さんぜんえん) です。

MINI DIALOGUE 4

A: Sorry, but we're full for today.
Sumimasen ga, kyō wa manseki dess.
すみませんが、今日 (きょう) は満席 (まんせき) です。

B: How about tomorrow?
Ashita wa dō dess ka?
明日 (あした) はどうですか？

A: Tomorrow is all right.
Ashita wa daijōbu dess.
明日 (あした) は大丈夫 (だいじょうぶ) です。

B: Well, then please make it for tomorrow.
Dewa, ashita de o-negai shimahss.
では、明日 (あした) でお願 (ねが) いします。

HOTEL FACILITIES

front desk; reception desk
furonto
フロント

lobby
robii
ロビー

hall; corridor
rōka
廊下 (ろうか)

elevator
erebētā
エレベーター

stairs
kaidan
階段 (かいだん)

dining hall
shokudō
食堂 (しょくどう)

bath (communal bath)
o-furo
お風呂 (ふろ)

RESERVATIONS AND CHECK-IN

room
heya
部屋 (へや)

single room
shinguru-rūmu
シングルルーム

double room
daburu-rūmu
ダブルルーム

twin room
tsuin
ツイン

bathroom
basu-rūmu
バスルーム

room with a bathroom
basu-tsuki no heya
バス付 (つ) きの部屋
(へや)

overnight stay
ip-paku
1泊 (いっぱく)

two-night stay
ni-haku
2泊 (にはく)

three-night stay
san-paku
3泊 (さんぱく)

cheap
yasui
安 (やす) い

better
motto ii
もっといい

view **nagame** 眺 (なが) め	ice **kōri** 氷 (こおり)	four people **yo-nin** 4人 (よにん)
key **kagi** 鍵 (かぎ)	three people **san-nin** 3人 (さんにん)	five people **go-nin** 5人 (ごにん)

EXAMPLES

We'll stay two nights.
Ni-haku shimahss.
2泊 (にはく) します。

Do you have a cheaper room?
Motto yasui heya wa arimahss ka?
もっと安 (やす) い部屋 (へや) はありますか?

Do you have a room with a better view?
Motto nagame no ii heya wa arimahss ka?
もっと眺 (なが) めのいい部屋 (へや) はありますか?

May I have some ice please?
Kōri wo kudasai.
氷 (こおり) をください。

CHECK-OUT

bill	no charge	tax
o-kanjō	**muryō**	**zeikin**
お勘定 (かんじょう)	無料 (むりょう)	税金 (ぜいきん)
charge	service charge	receipt
ryōkin	**sābisu-ryō**	**ryōshūsho**
料金 (りょうきん)	サービス料 (りょう)	領収書 (りょうしゅうしょ)

EXAMPLES

What is the price for one person?
Ryokin wa hitori ikura desska?
料金 (りょうきん) は一人 (ひとり) いくらですか?

OTHERS

wake me (up)	have this laundered	heater
okoshite kudasai	**kore wo sentaku shite-morau**	**danbō; hiitā**
起 (お) こしてください	これを洗濯 (せんたく) してもらう	暖房 (だんぼうそうち); ヒーター
mail		
yūbin	air conditioner	not work very well
郵便 (ゆうびん)	**reibō; kūrā; eakon**	**chōshi ga yokunai**
	冷房 (れいぼう); クーラー; エアコン	調子 (ちょうし) がよくない
stamp		
kitte		
切手 (きって)		

EXAMPLES

Please wake me at 8:oo.
Hachi-ji ni okoshite kudasai.
8時 (はちじ) に起 (お) こしてください。

Please put this in the mail.
Kore wo yūbin de dashite kudasai.
これを郵便 (ゆうびん) で出 (だ) してください。

Do you have stamps?
Kitte wa arimahss ka?
切手 (きって) はありますか?

Can I have this laundered?
Kore wo sentaku shitemorau koto wa dekimahss ka?
これを洗濯 (せんたく) してもらうことはできますか?

The air conditioner does not work very well.
Eakon no chōshi ga yokunai dess.
エアコンの調子 (ちょうし) がよくないです。

CHAPTER 17

Describing Your Travel Plans

When you speak Japanese, use short, easy phrases (which are also easier to re-member). Try to simplify your language; for example, rather than trying to say "I intend to spend time looking at old Japanese Buddhist temples," say "I'll see temples." That becomes simply **O-tera wo mimahss**. We'll learn how to describe your plans in the present and future tense, and then later, in Chapter 21, learn how to tell others what we did.

WORDS & EXPRESSIONS

tomorrow **ashita** 明日 (あした)	in Kyoto; at Kyoto **Kyōto de** 京都 (きょうと) で	Buddhist temple **o-tera** お寺 (てら)
Kyoto **Kyōto** 京都 (きょうと)	what **nani** 何 (なに	see **mimahss** 見 (み) ます
to Kyoto **Kyōto e** 京都 (きょうと) へ	[object particle] **wo** を	famous **yūmei na** 有名 (ゆうめい) な
go **ikimahss** 行 (い) きます	do **shimahss** します	garden **niwa** 庭 (にわ)

photographs	postcard	souvenir	to the park
shashin	**e-hagaki**	**o-miyage**	**kōen made**
写真 (しゃしん)	絵葉書 (えはがき)	お土産 (みやげ)	公園 (こうえん) まで

take	buy	park	walk
torimahss	**kaimahss**	**kōen**	**arukimahss**
撮 (と) ります	買 (か) います	公園 (こうえん)	歩 (ある) きます

EXAMPLES

Tomorrow I'll go to Kyoto.
Ashita Kyōto e ikimahss.
明日 (あした) 京都 (きょうと) へ行 (い) きます。

What will you do in Kyoto?
Kyōto de nani wo shimahss ka?
京都 (きょうと) で何 (なに) をしますか？

I'll see temples.
O-tera wo mimahss.
お寺 (てら) を見 (み) ます。

I'll go to a famous temple.
Yūmei na o-tera e ikimahss.
有名 (ゆうめい) なお寺 (てら) へ行 (い) きます。

I'll see famous gardens.
Yūmei na niwa wo mimahss.
有名 (ゆうめい) な庭 (にわ) を (み) 見ます。

I'll take some photos.
Shashin wo torimahss.
写真 (しゃしん) を撮 (と) ります。

I'll take a lot of photos of temples in Kyoto.
Kyōto de o-tera no shashin wo takusan torimahss.
京都 (きょうと) でお寺 (てら) の写真 (しゃしん) をたくさん撮 (と) ります。

I'll buy some postcards.
E-hagaki wo kaimahss.
絵葉書 (えはがき) を買 (か) います。

I'll buy some postcards at the temple.
O-tera de e-hagaki wo kaimahss.
お寺 (てら) で絵葉書 (えはがき) を買 (か) います。

I'll walk to the park.
Kōen made arukimahss.
公園 (こうえん) まで歩 (ある) きます。

ENCHANTING KYOTO

Every visitor to Japan should experience wandering around Kyoto's back streets. Wherever you turn, you'll discover a myriad shrines, temples, and traditional shops and residences. And in these back streets, you'll also find a peace and quiet that is rare in most other cities.

Because of its vast number of cultural treasures (there are over 1,700 shrines and 3,000 temples alone), Kyoto was not bombed in World War II. Thus, Kyoto remains Japan's cultural capital, a proud city that gave rise to one of the world's most refined civilizations.

EXPRESSIONS IN CONTEXT

 **MINI DIALOGUE 1**

A: I'll go to Kyoto tomorrow.
Ashita Kyōto e ikimahss.
明日 (あした) 京都 (きょうと) へ行 (い) きます。

B: What will you see in Kyoto?
Kyōto de nani wo mimahss ka?
京都 (きょうと) で何 (なに) を見 (み) ますか？

A: I'll see the famous gardens in Katsura-rikyu, Ryoan-ji, and Koke-dera.
Katsura-rikyū, Ryōan-ji, Koke-dera de yūmei na niwa wo mimahss.
桂離宮 (かつらりきゅう) 、龍安寺 (りょうあんじ) 、苔寺 (こけでら) で、
有名 (ゆうめい) な庭 (にわ) を見 (み) ます。

OTHER EXPRESSIONS

I'll go to the park tomorrow.
Ashita kōen e ikimahss.
明日 (あした) 公園 (こうえん) へ行 (い) きます。

I'll go to a famous garden tomorrow.
Ashita yūmei na niwa e ikimahss.
明日 (あした) 有名 (ゆうめい) な庭 (にわ) へ行 (い) きます。

What will you do?
Nani wo shimahss ka?
何 (なに) をしますか？

What will you see?
Nani wo mimahss ka?
何 (なに) を見 (み) ますか？

I'll see a famous park.
Yūmei na kōen wo mimahss.
有名 (ゆうめい) な公園 (こうえん) を見 (み) ます。

I'll walk to the park.
Kōen made arukimahss.
公園 (こうえん) まで歩 (ある) きます。

I'll take some photographs in the park.
Kōen de shashin wo torimahss.
公園 (こうえん) で写真 (しゃしん) を撮 (と) ります。

 **MINI DIALOGUE 2**

A: **What will you buy?**
   Nani wo kaimahss ka?
   何 (なに) を買 (か) いますか？

B: **I'll buy some souvenirs.**
   O-miyage wo kaimahss.
   お土産 (みやげ) を買 (か) います。

LEISURE ACTIVITIES

magazine
zasshi
雑誌 (ざっし)

radio
rajio
ラジオ

to the hotel
hoteru e
ホテルへ

book
hon
本 (ほん)

watch
miru/mirimahss
見 (み) る/見 (み) ます

return
kaeru/kaerimahss
帰 (かえ) る/帰 (かえ) ります

newspaper
shinbun
新聞 (しんぶん)

listen
kiku/kikimahss
聞 (き) く/聞 (き) きます

orange juice
orenji-jūsu
オレンジジュース

read
yomu/yomimahss
読 (よ) む/読 (よ) みます

letter
tegami
手紙 (てがみ)

early
hayaku
早 (はや) く

television
terebi
テレビ

write
kaku/kakimahss
書 (か) く/書 (か) きます

late
osoku
遅 (おそ) く

EXAMPLES

I'll read a magazine.
Zasshi wo yomimahss.
雑誌 (ざっし) を読 (よ) みます。

I'll listen to the radio.
Rajio wo kikimahss.
ラジオを聞 (き) きます。

I'll write a postcard.
E-hagaki wo kakimahss.
絵葉書 (えはがき) を書 (か) きます。

I'll return to the hotel.
Hoteru e kaerimahss.
ホテルへ帰 (かえ) ります。

I'll drink orange juice.
Orenji-jūsu wo nomimahss.
オレンジジュースを飲 (の) みます。

I'll get up early.
Hayaku okimahss.
早 (はや) く起 (お) きます。

I'll go to bed late.
Osoku nemahss.
遅 (おそ) く寝 (ね) ます。

CHAPTER 18
Expressing What You Want

Remember that communicating is your objective. Don't worry if your particles are wrong or your word order is incorrect. If you're unsure about a particle, simply skip over it. The truth is that many Japanese drop particles in conversation, so it's not a problem if you do too.

WORDS & EXPRESSIONS

Japanese doll
Nihon ningyō
日本人形 (にほんにんぎょう)

[subject particle]
ga
が

want
hoshii
ほしい

Japanese inn
ryokan
旅館 (りょかん)

like
suki
好 (す) き

hotel
hoteru
ホテル

[subject particle, frequently used in negative sentences]
wa
は

don't like
suki dewa arimasen
好 (す) きではありません

what
nani
何 (なに)

[direct object particle]
wo
を

want to do
shi-tai
したい

sumo [traditional Japanese wrestling]
sumō
相撲 (すもう)

want to see **mi-tai** 見 (み) たい	woodblock print **hanga** 版画 (はんが)	slowly **yukkuri** ゆっくり
to Mount Fuji **Fuji-san e** 富士山 (ふじさん) へ	want to buy **kai-tai** 買 (か) いたい	please speak **hanashite kudasai** 話 (はな) してください
want to go **iki-tai** 行 (い) きたい	pottery **seto-mono** 瀬戸物 (せともの)	picture **shashin** 写真 (しゃしん)
please take **totte kudasai** 撮 (と) ってください		

EXAMPLES

I want a Japanese doll.
Nihon ningyō ga hoshii dess.
日本人形 (にほんにんぎょう) がほしいです。

I like Japanese inns.
Ryokan ga suki dess.
旅館 (りょかん) が好 (す) きです。

I don't like hotels.
Hoteru wa suki dewa arimasen.
ホテルは好 (す) きではありません。

What do you want to do?
Nani wo shi-tai dess ka?
何 (なに) をしたいですか?

I want to see sumo.
Sumō wo mi-tai dess.
相撲 (すもう) を見 (み) たいです。

I want to go to Mount Fuji.
Fuji-san e iki-tai dess.
富士山 (ふじさん) へ行 (い) きたいです。

I want to buy woodblock prints.
Hanga wo kai-tai dess.
版画 (はんが) を買 (か) いたいです。

Please speak slowly.
Yukkuri hanashite kudasai.
ゆっくり話 (はな) してください。

Please take a picture.
Shashin wo totte kudasai.
写真 (しゃしん) を撮 (と) ってください。

MOUNT FUJI

Japan's most revered mountain, Mount Fuji, is called **Fuji-san** in Japanese. **San**, which here means "mountain" and not "Mr.", is used with other Japanese mountains like **Asosan** in Kyushu and **Ontakesan** in Nagano.

At 12,389 feet or 3,776 meters, Mount Fuji is Japan's highest mountain, and although it last erupted in 1707, it's classified as an active volcano. From the bullet train, you can get a good view of Mount Fuji's superb conical shape. The adventurous can climb it; people of all ages climb Mount Fuji, mostly to see the breathtaking sunrise over the Pacific Ocean.

EXPRESSIONS IN CONTEXT

 **MINI DIALOGUE 1**

A: **What do you want to buy?**
Nani wo kai-tai dess ka?
何 (なに) を買 (か) いたいですか？

B: **I want to buy a Japanese doll.**
Nihon ningyō wo kai-tai dess.
日本人形 (にほんにんぎょう) を買 (か) いたいです。

OTHER EXPRESSIONS

I want to buy some pottery.
Seto-mono wo kai-tai dess.
瀬戸物 (せともの) を買 (か) いたいです。

I want a woodblock print.
Hanga ga hoshii dess.
版画 (はんが) がほしいです。

 **MINI DIALOGUE 2**

A: **What do you like?**
Nani ga suki dess ka?
何 (なに) が好 (す) きですか？

B: **I like sumo.**
Sumō ga suki dess.
相撲 (すもう) が好 (す) きです。

OTHER EXPRESSIONS

I don't like woodblock prints.
Hanga wa suki dewa arimasen.
版画 (はんが) は好 (す) きではありません。

 **MINI DIALOGUE 3**

A: What do you want to do?
Nani wo shi-tai dess ka?
何 (なに) をしたいですか？

B: I want to go to Kyoto.
Kyōto e iki-tai dess.
京都 (きょうと) へ行 (い) きたいです。

 **MINI DIALOGUE 4**

A: What do you want to see?
Nani wo mi-tai dess ka?
何 (なに) を見 (み) たいですか？

B: I want to see Mount Fuji.
Fuji-san wo mi-tai dess.
富士山 (ふじさん) を見 (み) たいです。

OTHER EXPRESSIONS

I want to see sumo.
Sumō wo mi-tai dess.
相撲 (すもう) を見 (み) たいです。

ADDITIONAL WORDS & EXPRESSIONS

sports
supōtsu
スポーツ

physical exercise
undō
運動 (うんどう)

I need to do some
exercise.
Undō wo shi-tai dess.
運動 (うんどう) をした
いです。

ocean
umi
海 (うみ)

lake
mizuumi
湖 (みずうみ)

mountain
yama
山 (やま)

mountain climbing
yama-nobori
山登 (やまのぼ) り

hiking
haikingu
ハイキング

camping
kyanpu
キャンプ

go (board game played
with black and white
stones)
go
碁 (ご)

mahjong
mājan
麻雀 (マージャン)

painting
e
絵 (え)

sculpture
chōkoku
彫刻 (ちょうこく)

antique
kottō-hin
骨董品 (こっとうひん)

EXAMPLES

I want to go camping.
Kyanpu wo shi-tai dess.
キャンプをしたいです。

I'm looking for some antiques.
Kottō-hin wo sagashite imahss.
骨董品 (こっとうひん) を探 (さが) しています。

Excuse me. May I take a picture?
Sumimasen. Shashin wo totte ii dess ka?
すみません。写真 (しゃしん) を撮 (と) っていいですか?

May I take your picture?
Anata no shashin wo totte ii dess ka?
あなたの写真 (しゃしん) を撮 (と) っていいですか?

Excuse me. Please take a picture of me/us.
Sumimasen. Shashin wo totte kudasai/ itadakemahss ka?
すみません。写真 (しゃしん) を撮 (と) ってください/いただけますか?

CHAPTER 19
Shopping

Shop clerks in Japan are very polite and eager to help, and if you speak slowly and gesture, you shouldn't have problems being understood. Of course, understanding what they are saying is a different story. If you're unsure of a price, have a clerk write it down. They might also put in the numbers on a calculator and show it to you.

WORDS & EXPRESSIONS

how much
ikura
いくら

this
kore
これ

2,000 yen
ni-sen-en
2,000円 (にせんえん)

10,000 yen
ichi-man-en
1万円 (いちまんえん)

this watch
kono tokei
この時計 (とけい)

43,000 yen
yon-man san-zen-en
43,000円 (よんまんさん
ぜんえん)

please; please give
kudasai
ください

big
ōkii
大 (おお) きい

more
motto
もっと

bigger
motto ōkii
もっと大 (おお) きい

big one
ōkii-no
大 (おお) きいの

please show
misete kudasai
見 (み) せてください

inexpensive **yasui** 安 (やす) い	please say **itte kudasai** 言 (い) ってください	price **nedan** 値段 (ねだん)
inexpensive one **yasui-no** 安 (やす) いの	in English **Ei-go de** 英語 (えいご) で	please write **kaite kudasai** 書 (か) いてください
different one **hoka-no** 他 (ほか) の	please speak **hanashite kudasai** 話 (はな) してください	
once more **mō ichido** もう一度 (いちど)	in Japanese **Nihon-go de** 日本語 (にほんご) で	

EXAMPLES

How much is it?
Ikura dess ka?
いくらですか？

How much is this?
Kore wa ikura dess ka?
これはいくらですか？

It's 2,000 yen.
Ni-sen-en dess.
2,000円 (にせんえん) です。

This watch is 43,000 yen.
Kono tokei wa yon-man san-zen-en dess.
この時計 (とけい) は43,000円 (よんまんさんぜんえん) です。

Please give me this. (I'll take this.)
Kore wo kudasai.
これをください。

Please show me a bigger one (when you're looking for a larger size for clothes).
Motto ōkii-no wo misete kudasai.
もっと大 (おお) きいのを見 (み) せてください。

Please show me an inexpensive one (for souvenirs/clothes/things you're buying).
Yasui-no wo misete kudasai.
安 (やす) いのを見 (み) せてください。

Please say it once more.
Mō ichido itte kudasai.
もう一度 (いちど) 言 (い) ってください。

Please speak in English.
Ei-go de hanashite kudasai.
英語 (えいご) で話 (はな) してください。

Please write down the price.
Nedan wo kaite kudasai.
値段 (ねだん) を書 (か) いてください。

FOLK-ART HANDICRAFTS

Mingei-hin, colorful folk-art handicrafts, make perfect gifts or souvenirs from Japan. As you travel, keep an eye out for local specialties. Tokyo, for example, is famous for its glass wind chimes (**fūrin**), Kyoto for its folding paper fans (**sensu**), and Tohoku for its delicately hand-painted wooden dolls (**kokeshi**). In most cities, **mingei-hin** are sold at small shops around tourist attractions and train stations. **Mingei** stores in larger cities have wonderful selections and fair prices, but they're often hard to find. It's a good idea to ask for directions.

EXPRESSIONS IN CONTEXT

 **MINI DIALOGUE 1**

A: How much is this?
Kore wa ikura dess ka?
これはいくらですか？

B: It's 2,000 yen.
Ni-sen-en dess.
2,000円（にせんえん）です。

A: How much is the big one?
Ōkii-no wa ikura dess ka?
大（おお）きいのはいくらですか？

B: It's 3,000 yen.
San-zen-en dess.
3,000円（さんぜんえん）です。

A: Please show me this.
Kore wo misete kudasai.
これを見（み）せてください。

OTHER EXPRESSIONS

Please show me a different one.
Hoka-no wo misete kudasai.
他 (ほか) のを見 (み) せてください。

Please show me once more.
Mō ichido misete kudasai.
もう一度 (いちど) 見 (み) せてください。

 MINI DIALOGUE 2

A: How much is this watch?
   Kono tokei wa ikura dess ka?
   この時計 (とけい) はいくらですか?

B: It's 40,000 yen.
   Yon-man-en dess.
   4万円 (よんまんえん) です。

A: Please say it once more.
   Mō ichido itte kudasai.
   もう一度 (いちど)言(い)ってください。

B: It's 40,000 yen.
   Yon-man-en dess.
   4万円 (よんまんえん) です。

A: Please give me this. (I'll take this.)
   Kore wo kudasai.
   これをください。

OTHER EXPRESSIONS

It's 10,000 yen.
Ichi-man-en dess.
1万円 (いちまんえん) です。

Please write this.
Kore wo kaite kudasai.
これを書 (か) いてください。

Please give me this watch.
Kono tokei wo kudasai.
この時計 (とけい) をください。

Please give me this inexpensive one.
Kono yasui-no wo kudasai.
この安 (やす) いのをください。

USEFUL ADJECTIVES

small
chiisai
小 (ちい) さい

expensive
takai
高 (たか) い

small (for clothes)
esu
S (エス)

medium (for clothes)
emu
M (エム)

large (for clothes)
eru
L (エル)

extra large (for clothes)
eru-eru; ekkusu-eru
LL (エルエル); XL (エック
スエル)

light
karui
軽 (かる) い

heavy
omoi
重 (おも) い

round
marui
丸 (まる) い

square
shikakui
四角 (しかく) い

bright
azayaka-na
鮮 (あざ) やかな

subdued; refined
jimi-na
地味 (じみ) な

flashy; gaudy
hade-na
派手 (はで) な

beautiful
utsukushii
美 (うつく) しい

pretty
kirei-na
きれいな

old/vintage
furui
古 (ふる) い

new
atarashii
新 (あたら) しい

traditional
dentō-teki-na
伝統的 (でんとうてき) な

JAPANESE PRODUCTS

silk
kinu
絹 (きぬ)

cloth; textile
ori-mono
織物 (おりもの)

electrical goods
denka-seihin
電化製品 (でんかせいひん)

lacquerware
nuri-mono
塗 (ぬ) り物 (もの)

pottery
seto-mono
瀬戸物 (せともの)

pearl
shinju
真珠 (しんじゅ)

folding fan
sensu
扇子 (せんす)

folk-art handicraft
mingei-hin
民芸品 (みんげいひん)

cloth used for wrapping things
furoshiki
風呂敷 (ふろしき)

chinaware
tōjiki
陶磁器 (とうじき)

hanging scroll; hanging picture
kake-mono
掛 (か) け物 (もの)

kimono
kimono
着物 (きもの)

light cotton kimono
yukata
浴衣 (ゆかた)

lantern
chōchin
提灯 (ちょうちん)

traditional handmade paper
washi
和紙 (わし)

woodblock print
hanga
版画 (はんが)

ARTICLES OF CLOTHING

shirt
shatsu
シャツ

T-shirt
tii-shatsu
T (ティー) シャツ

underwear
shitagi
下着 (したぎ)

undershirt
shatsu
シャツ

undershort
pantsu
パンツ

sweater
seta
セーター

cardigan
kādegan
カーデガン

vest
besuto
ベスト

sweatshirt
torēnā; suetto
トレーナー; スエット

jacket/coat **uwagi** 上着 (うわぎ)	pants (trousers) **pantsu** パンツ	sock(s) **kutsushita** 靴下 (くつした)
coat **kōto** コート	skirt **sukāto** スカート	hat; cap **bōshi** 帽子 (ぼうし)
raincoat **reinkōto** レインコート	dress (one-piece suit) **wanpiisu** ワンピース	gloves **tebukuro** 手袋 (てぶくろ)

OTHERS

a little; a moment **chotto** ちょっと	please send **okutte kudasai** 送 (おく) ってください	gift-wrap **okuri-mono yō ni tsu-tsumu** 贈 (おく) り物 (もの) 用 (よう) に包 (つつ) む
please wait **matte kudasai** 待 (ま) ってください	please wrap **tsutsunde kudasai** 包 (つつ) んでください	

EXAMPLES

Please wait a moment.
Chotto matte kudasai.
ちょっと待 (ま) ってください。

Please send this.
Kore wo okutte kudasai.
これを送 (おく) ってください。

Please wrap this.
Kore wo tsutsunde kudasai.
これを包 (つつ) んでください。

Please gift-wrap it.
Sore wo okuri-mono yō ni tsutsunde kudasai.
これを贈 (おく) り物 (もの) 用 (よう) に包 (つつ) んでください。

CHAPTER 20
Talking About the Weather

The Japanese believe they discuss the weather more than other people do. True or not, the weather offers you a good way to start a conversation. One thing is certain; the Japanese will be curious to know what type of weather you have in your part of the world.

WORDS & EXPRESSIONS

today
kyō
今日 (きょう)

good; nice
ii
いい

weather
tenki
天気 (てんき)

Isn't it?
Ne.
ね。

tomorrow
ashita
明日 (あした)

how
dō
どう

will be; will probably be
deshō
でしょう

weekend
shūmatsu
週末 (しゅうまつ)

probably
tabun
たぶん

It'll probably...
tabun... deshō
たぶん でしょう

rain; rainy
ame
雨 (あめ)

cold (temperature)
samui
寒 (さむ) い

yesterday
kinō
昨日 (きのう)

bad weather
warui tenki
悪 (わる) い天気 (てんき)

was
deshita
でした

Hiroshima (See PRE-
FECTURES IN JAPAN in
Chapter 2)
Hiroshima
広島 (ひろしま)

hot day
atsui hi
暑 (あつ) い日 (ひ)

fine weather
hare
晴 (は) れ

warm
atatakai
暖 (あたた) かい

cool
suzushii
涼 (すず) しい

EXAMPLES

It's nice weather today, isn't it?
Kyō wa ii tenki dess ne?
今日 (きょう) はいい天気 (てんき) ですね?

It is, isn't it?/That's right.
Sō dess ne.
そうですね。

How will the weather be tomorrow?
Ashita no tenki wa dō naru deshō ka?
明日 (あした) の天気 (てんき) はどうなるでしょうか?

What will the weather be like tomorrow?
Ashita wa don-na tenki ni narimahss ka?
明日 (あした) はどんな天気 (てんき) になりますか?

It'll probably be rainy.
Tabun, ame deshō.
たぶん、雨 (あめ) でしょう。

It'll probably be cold.
Samui deshō.
寒 (さむ) いでしょう。

The weather was bad yesterday.
Kinō wa warui tenki deshita.
昨日 (きのう) は悪 (わる) い天気 (てんき) でした。

It was a hot day.
Atsui hi deshita.
暑 (あつ) い日 (ひ) でした。

The weather was fine in Hiroshima.
Hiroshima wa hare deshita.
広島 (ひろしま) は晴 (は) れでした。

Today is warm, isn't it?
Kyō wa atatakai dess ne?
今日 (きょう) は暖 (あたた) かいですね?

JAPANESE SEASONS

Japan has four major seasons—spring, summer, fall, and winter—with rainy periods between spring and summer, and summer and fall. During the fall rainy period, typhoons bring torrential rainfalls to all of the country except Hokkaido. Although the part of Japan bordering the Pacific Ocean has little snow in winter, areas like Kanazawa along the Japan Sea have heavy snowfalls that isolate rural villages. The change in landscape is dramatic. From Kyoto, which may have no snow on the ground, a train ride through a series of tunnels will take you to the heart of snow country in a matter of minutes.

EXPRESSIONS IN CONTEXT

 **MINI DIALOGUE 1**

A: **It's nice weather today, isn't it?**
Kyō wa ii tenki dess ne?
今日 (きょう) はいい天気 (てんき) ですね?

B: **It certainly is.**
Sō dess ne.
そうですね。

OTHER EXPRESSIONS

Cool, isn't it?
Suzushii dess ne.
涼（すず）しいですね。

Hot, isn't it?
Atsui dess ne.
暑（あつ）いですね。

 **MINI DIALOGUE 2**

A: **How will it be this weekend?**
   Shūmatsu no tenki wa dō deshō ka?
   週末（しゅうまつ）の天気（てんき）はどうでしょうか？

B: **Well, it'll probably be fair.**
   Tabun, hare deshō.
   たぶん、晴（は）れでしょう。

OTHER EXPRESSIONS

It'll be nice.
Ii tenki deshō.
いい天気（てんき）でしょう。

 **MINI DIALOGUE 3**

A: **How was the weather like yesterday?**
   Kinō wa dō deshita ka?
   昨日（きのう）はどうでしたか？

B: **The weather was bad.**
   Warui tenki deshita.
   悪（わる）い天気（てんき）でした。

OTHER EXPRESSIONS

It was a cold day.
Samui hi deshita.
寒 (さむ) い日 (ひ) でした。

It was rainy.
Ame deshita.
雨 (あめ) でした。

 **MINI DIALOGUE 4**

A: **How was Hiroshima?**
   Hiroshima wa dō deshita ka?
   広島 (ひろしま) はどうでしたか？

B: **The weather was fine.**
   Hare deshita.
   晴 (は) れでした。

OTHER EXPRESSIONS

The weather was nice.
Ii tenki deshita.
いい天気 (てんき) でした。

MINI DIALOGUE 5

A: **Was the weather bad yesterday?**
   Kinō wa warui tenki deshita ka?
   昨日 (きのう) は悪 (わる)
   い天気 (てんき) でしたか？

B: **No, it was fine.**
   Iie, hare deshita.
   いいえ、晴 (は) れでした。

OTHER EXPRESSIONS

It was a warm day.
Atatakai hi deshita.
暖 (あたた) かい日 (ひ) でした。

ADDITIONAL WORDS & EXPRESSIONS

climate
kikō
気候 (きこう)

weather forecast
tenki-yohō
天気予報 (てんきよほう)

weather bureau
kishō-dai
気象台 (きしょうだい)

temperature
ondo
温度 (おんど)

degree
do
度 (ど)

Fahrenheit
Kashi
華氏 (かし)

70 degrees Fahrenheit
Kashi nana-jū-do
華氏 (かし) 70度 (ななじ
ゅうど)

snow
yuki
雪 (ゆき)

fall (rain, snow)
furimahss
降 (ふ) ります

fog
kiri
霧 (きり)

shower
niwaka-ame
にわか雨 (あめ)

wind
kaze
風 (かぜ)

Celsius
Sesshi
摂氏 (せっし)

20 degrees Celsius
Sesshi ni-jū-do
摂氏 (せっし) 20度 (にじ
ゅうど)

storm
arashi
嵐 (あらし)

typhoon
taifū
台風 (たいふう)

thunder
kaminari
雷 (かみなり)

lightning
inazuma
稲妻 (いなずま)

cloudy
kumori
曇 (くも) り

humid
mushi-atsui
蒸 (む) し暑 (あつ) い

umbrella
kasa
傘 (かさ)

earthquake
jishin
地震 (じしん)

EXAMPLES

According to the weather forecast, tomorrow will be rainy.
Tenki-yohō ni yoru to, ashita wa ame dess.
天気予報 (てんきよほう) によると、明日 (あした) は雨 (あめ) です。

It snows.
Yuki ga furimahss.
雪 (ゆき) が降 (ふ) ります。

CHAPTER 21
Describing What You Did

In this chapter we will learn how to tell others what you did on your travels around Japan. If a Japanese word ends in **mashita,** you can be almost certain that the word is a verb in its past tense. For example, the present tense of the verb "to go" is **ikimahss** and the past tense is **ikimashita.** The present tense of the verb "to do" is **shimahss** and the past tense is **shimashita.** There are few exceptions to this rule.

WORDS & EXPRESSIONS

yesterday
kinō
昨日 (きのう)

where
doko
どこ

to
e
へ

where to
doko e
どこへ

went
ikimashita
行 (い) きました

Nara
Nara
奈良 (なら)

to Nara
Nara e
奈良 (なら) へ

in Nara
Nara de
奈良 (なら) で

what
nani
何 (なに)

did
shimashita
しました

large statue of Buddha
daibutsu
大仏 (だいぶつ)

saw
mimashita
見 (み) ました

park **kōen** 公園 (こうえん)	of **no** の	souvenir **omiyage** お土産 (みやげ)
walked **arukimashita** 歩 (ある) きました	photo of deer **shika no shashin** 鹿 (しか) の写真 (しゃしん)	bought **kaimashita** 買 (か) いました
deer (Nara is famous for its deer.) **shika** 鹿 (しか)	took **torimashita** 撮 (と) りました	

EXAMPLES

Where did you go yesterday?
Kinō doko e ikimashita ka?
昨日 (きのう) どこへ行 (い) きましたか？

I went to Nara.
Nara e ikimashita.
奈良 (なら) へ行 (い) きました。

What did you do in Nara?
Nara de nani wo shimashita ka?
奈良 (なら) で何 (なに) をしましたか？

I saw the large statue of Buddha in Nara.
Nara de daibutsu wo mimashita.
奈良 (なら) で大仏 (だいぶつ) を見 (み) ました。

I walked to the park.
Kōen made arukimashita.
公園 (こうえん) まで歩 (ある) きました。

I took some photos.
Shashin wo torimashita.
写真 (しゃしん) を撮 (と) りました。

I took some photos of deer.
Shika no shashin wo torimashita.
鹿（しか）の写真（しゃしん）を撮（と）りました。

I bought souvenirs.
O-miyage wo kaimashita.
お土産（みやげ）を買（か）いました。

EXPRESSIONS IN CONTEXT

 MINI DIALOGUE 1

A: Where did you go?
    Doko e ikimashita ka?
    どこへ行（い）きましたか？

B: I went to Kyoto.
    Kyōto e ikimashita.
    京都（きょうと）へ行（い）きました。

OTHER EXPRESSIONS

I went to a Buddhist temple.
O-tera e ikimashita.
お寺（てら）へ行（い）きました。

I went to the park.
Kōen e ikimashita.
公園（こうえん）へ行（い）きました。

 MINI DIALOGUE 2

A: What did you see in Nara?
    Nara de nani wo mimashita ka?
    奈良（なら）で何（なに）を見（み）ましたか？

B: I saw Buddhist temples.
O-tera wo mimashita.
お寺 (てら) を見 (み) ました。

OTHER EXPRESSIONS

I saw the park.
Kōen wo mimashita.
公園 (こうえん) を見 (み) ました。

I saw deer.
Shika wo mimashita.
鹿 (しか) を見 (み) ました。

 MINI DIALOGUE 3

A: What did you do?
 Nani wo shimashita ka?
 何 (なに) をしましたか?

B: I took some photos.
 Shashin wo torimashita.
 写真 (しゃしん) を撮 (と) りました。

OTHER EXPRESSIONS

What did you see?
Nani wo mimashita ka?
何 (なに) を見 (み) ましたか?

Did you see Buddhist temples?
O-tera wo mimashita ka?
お寺 (てら) を見 (み) ましたか?

 MINI DIALOGUE 4

A: Did you take photos?
 Shashin wo torimashita ka?
 写真 (しゃしん) を撮 (と) りましたか?

B: Yes, I did. I took photos of the deer.
   Hai, torimashita. Shika no shashin wo torimashita.
   はい、撮（と）りました。鹿（しか）の写真（しゃしん）を撮（と）りました。

 MINI DIALOGUE 5

A: What did you buy?
   Nani wo kaimashita ka?
   何（なに）を買（か）いましたか？

B: I bought some souvenirs.
   Omiyage wo kaimashita.
   お土産（みやげ）を買（か）いました。

ADDITIONAL WORDS & EXPRESSIONS

college; university
daigaku
大学（だいがく）

library
tosho-kan
図書館（としょかん）

movie theater
eiga-kan
映画館（えいがかん）

theater
gekijō
劇場（げきじょう）

gallery
garō
画廊（がろう）

stadium
sutajiamu
スタジアム

public square
hiro-ba
広場（ひろば）

historical site
shiseki
史跡（しせき）

monument
kinen-hi
記念碑（きねんひ）

statue
zō
像（ぞう）

regional specialty
meisan
名産（めいさん）

place of interest (tourist attraction)
meisho
名所（めいしょ）

admission ticket
nyūjō-ken
入場券（にゅうじょうけん）

admission fee
nyūjō-ryō
入場料（にゅうじょうりょう）

EXAMPLES

I went to a historical site.
Shiseki e ikimashita.
史跡 (しせき) へ行 (い) きました。

Are there any tourist attractions around here?
Kono hen ni meisho wa arimahss ka?
このへんに名所 (めいしょ) はありますか?

What product is this area famous for?
Kono hen no meisan wa nan dess ka?
このへんの名産 (めいさん) は何 (なん) ですか?

I bought an admission ticket.
Nyūjō-ken wo kaimashita.
入場券 (にゅうじょうけん) を買 (か) いました。

How much is the admission fee?
Nyūjō-ryō wa ikura dess ka?
入場料 (にゅうじょうりょう) はいくらですか?

ADDITIONAL PLACES OF INTEREST

Meiji Shrine
Meiji Jingū
明治神宮（めいじじん
ぐう）

Sensoji Temple
Sen-sōji
浅草寺（せんそうじ）

Tokyo Sky Tree
Tōkyō Sukai Tsurii
東京（とうきょう）スカイ
ツリー

Tokyo Tower
Tōkyō Tawā
東京（とうきょう）タワー

Shinjuku Gyoen
National Garden
Shinjuku Gyoen
新宿（しんじゅく）
御苑（ぎょえん）

Kiyomizudera Temple
(lit. Pure Water Temple)
Kiyomizu-dera
清水寺（きよみずでら）

Kabukiza Theater
Kabukiza
歌舞伎座（かぶきざ）

Mount Fuji
Fujisan
富士山（ふじさん）

Toshogu Shrine
Nikkō Tōshōgū
日光東照宮（にっこうとう
しょうぐう）

Tokyo Disneyland
Tōkyō Dizunii rando
東京（とうきょう）ディズ
ニーランド

Ise Shrine
Ise Jingū
伊勢神宮（いせじんぐう）

The Golden Pavilion
Kinkaku-ji
金閣寺（きんかくじ）

The Silver Pavilion
Ginkaku-ji
銀閣寺（ぎんかくじ）

Toji Temple
Tō-ji
東寺（とうじ）

Nijo Castle
Nijōjō
二条城（にじょうじょう）

Todaiji Temple
Tōdai-ji
東大寺（とうだいじ）

Himeji Castle
Himeji-jō
姫路城（ひめじじょう）

Izumo Shrine
Izumo Taisha
出雲大社（いずもたいしゃ）

Mount Sakurajima
Sakurajima
桜島（さくらじま）

CHAPTER 22
Help!

If you need help as you're wandering about, go to a neighborhood "police box" (**kōban**), usually located near train or subway stations and on street corners. Look for a small building with a sign that says KOBAN or 交番. The policemen on duty will gladly assist you in any way, even if it's just helping with directions.

WORDS & EXPRESSIONS

Help! **Tasukete!** 助 (たす) けて！	on the train **densha ni** 電車 (でんしゃ) に	tablet **taburetto** タブレット
stole **nusumimashita** 盗 (ぬす) みました	camera **kamera** カメラ	way; road **michi** 道 (みち)
in trouble **komatte** 困 (こま) って	wallet **saifu** 財布 (さいふ)	lost (the way) **mayoimashita** 迷 (まよ) いました
ticket **kippu** 切符 (きっぷ)	passport **pasupōto** パスポート	hotel **hoteru** ホテル
lost **nakushimashita** なくしました	laptop **rappu toppu** ラップトップ	where **doko** どこ

don't know; can't find **wakarimasen** わかりません	please call **yonde kudasai** 呼 (よ) んでください	sick **guai ga warui** 具合 (ぐあい) が悪 (わる) い
here; this place **koko** ここ	English language **Ei-go** 英語 (えいご)	ambulance **kyūkyū-sha** 救急車 (きゅうきゅうしゃ)
telephone **denwa** 電話 (でんわ)	person who speaks **hanasu hito** 話 (はな) す人 (ひと)	

EXAMPLES

Please help me.
Tasukete kudasai.
助 (たす) けてください。

I'm in trouble.
Komatte imahss.
困 (こま) っています。

What happened?
Dō shimashita ka?
どうしましたか？

I lost my ticket.
Kippu wo nakushimashita.
切符 (きっぷ) をなくしました。

Somebody stole my bag.
Dareka ga watashi no kaban wo nusumimashita.
誰 (だれ) かが私 (わたし) のカバンを盗 (ぬす) みました。

I forgot my camera on the train.
Densha ni kamera wo wasuremashita.
電車 (でんしゃ) にカメラを忘 (わす) れました。

I lost my way.
Michi ni mayoimashita.
道 (みち) に迷 (まよ) いました。

I don't know where my hotel is.
Hoteru ga doko ka wakarimasen.
ホテルがどこかわかりません。

Where am I?
Koko wa doko dess ka?
ここはどこですか？

Where's a telephone?
Denwa wa doko dess ka?
電話 (でんわ) はどこですか？

Please call an ambulance.
Kyūkyū-sha wo yonde kudasai.
救急車 (きゅうきゅうしゃ)
を呼 (よ) んでください。

I'm sick.
Guai ga warui no dess.
具合 (ぐあい) が悪 (わる) いのです。

Please call a person who speaks English.
Ei-go wo hanasu hito wo yonde kudasai.
英語 (えいご) を話 (はな) す人 (ひと) を呼 (よ) んでください。

USEFUL TELEPHONE NUMBERS

For travel information in English, call the Tourist Information Center (TIC). In Tokyo, you'll find them at Tokyo Metropolitan Government Building (03-5321-3077), Keisei Ueno Station (03-3836-3471), and at Shinjuku Expressway Bus Terminal (03-6274-8192). In Kyoto, call (075) 343-0548; in Yokohama (045) 441-7300 and at Narita Airport, (0476) 34-5877 or (0476) 30-3383. The website of the Japan National Tourism Organization at http://www.jnto.go.jp.

For the police, dial 110 anywhere in the country. For reporting a fire or calling an ambulance, the number nationwide is 119.

EXPRESSIONS IN CONTEXT

 **MINI DIALOGUE 1**

A: Please help me.
Tasukete kudasai.
助 (たす) けてください。

B: What happened?
Dō shimashita ka?
どうしましたか？

A: I'm sick.
Guai ga warui no dess.
具合 (ぐあい) が悪 (わる) いのです。

 **MINI DIALOGUE 2**

A: I'm in trouble. Please help me.
Komatte imahss. Tasukete kudasai.
困 (こま) っています。助 (たす) けてください。

B: What happened?
Dō shimashita ka?
どうしましたか？

A: I lost my way.
Michi ni mayoimashita.
道 (みち) に迷 (まよ) いました。

OTHER EXPRESSIONS

Where's the hotel?
Hoteru wa doko dess ka?
ホテルはどこですか？

Where's a telephone?
Denwa wa doko dess ka?
電話 (でんわ) はどこですか？

I lost my ticket.
Kippu wo nakushimashita.
切符 (きっぷ) をなくしました。

I don't understand.
Wakarimasen.
わかりません。

Please call a person who speaks English.
Ei-go wo hanasu hito wo yonde kudasai.
英語 (えいご) を話 (はな) す人 (ひと) を呼 (よ) んでください。

HEALTH

doctor
isha
医者 (いしゃ)

English-speaking doctor
Ei-go wo hanasu isha
英語 (えいご) を話 (はな) す医者 (いしゃ)

hospital
byōin
病院 (びょういん)

nurse
kango-fu
看護婦 (かんごふ)

injection; shot
chūsha
注射 (ちゅうしゃ)

injury
kega
けが

thermometer
taion-kei
体温計 (たいおんけい)

fever
netsu
熱 (ねつ)

hurt
itai
痛 (いた) い

head
atama
頭 (あたま)

stomach
o-naka
お腹 (なか)

tooth
ha
歯 (は)

foot; leg
ashi
足 (あし) ／脚 (あし)

hand
te
手 (て)

swollen
harete imahss
腫 (は) れています

cold (flu)
kaze
風邪 (かぜ)

Chinese medicine
kanpō-yaku
漢方薬 (かんぽうやく)

blister
mame
マメ

medicine
kusuri
薬 (くすり)

diarrhea
geri
下痢 (げり)

cold medicine
kaze-gusuri
風邪薬 (かぜぐすり)

EXAMPLES

Please call a doctor.
Isha wo yonde kudasai.
医者 (いしゃ) を呼 (よ) んでください。

I have a fever.
Netsu ga arimahss.
熱 (ねつ) があります。

My head hurts.
Atama ga itai dess.
頭 (あたま) が痛 (いた) いです。

My foot is swollen.
Ashi ga harete imahss.
足 (あし) が腫 (は) れています。

I've developed a blister.
Mame ga dekimashita.
マメができました。

I've got diarrhea.
Geri wo shite imahss.
下痢 (げり) をしています。

I have a cold.
Kaze wo hiite imahss.
風邪 (かぜ) をひいています。

Do you have this medicine?
Kono kusuri wa arimahss ka?
この薬 (くすり) はありますか?

Do you have some medicine for me?
Nani-ka kusuri wa arimahss ka?
何（なに）か薬（くすり）はありますか？

OTHERS

money
o-kane
お金（かね）

passport
pasupōto
パスポート

credit card
kurejitto kādo
クレジットカード

ATM card
kyasshu kādo
キャッシュカード

JR Pass
Jei Āru Pass
ジェイアールパス

ID card
**mibun shōmeisho/
aidii kādo**
身分証明書（みぶんしょ
うめいしょ）／アイディー
カード

consulate
ryōji-kan
領事館（りょうじかん）

embassy
taishi-kan
大使館（たいしかん）

police station
keisatsu-sho
警察署（けいさつしょ）

driver's license
unten menkyoshō
運転免許証（うんてんめん
きょしょう）

police box
kōban
交番（こうばん）

thief
dorobō
泥棒（どろぼう）

pickpocket
suri
すり

EXAMPLES

I was robbed by a thief.
Dorobō ni nusumaremashita.
泥棒（どろぼう）に盗（ぬ）すまれました。

English-Japanese Dictionary

A

a little **chotto** ちょっと

a moment **shibaraku; chotto** しばらく; ちょっと

a.m. **gozen** 午前(ごぜん)

admission fee **nyūjō-ryō** 入場料(にゅうじょうりょう)

admission ticket **nyūjō-ken** 入場券(にゅうじょうけん)

adult **otona** 大人(おとな)

after... **...no ato (de)** …の後(あと)(で)

again **mata** また

Aichi (prefecture) **Aichi-ken** 愛知県(あいちけん)

air conditioner **reibō; kūrā; eakon** 冷房 (れいぼう); クーラー; エアコン

airport **kūkō** 空港(くうこう)

Akita (prefecture) **Akita-ken** 秋田県(あきたけん)

alarm clock **mezamashi-dokei** 目覚(めざ)まし時計(どけい)

all right **daijōbu** 大丈夫(だいじょうぶ)

alone; by onself **hitori de** 一人(ひとり)で

am **dess** です

am not **dewa arimasen** ではありません

ambulance **kyūkyū-sha** 救急車(きゅうきゅうしゃ)

American **Amerika-jin** アメリカ人(じん)

amusement park **yūen-chi** 遊園地(ゆうえんち)

anniversary **kinen-bi** 記念日(きねんび)

antique **kottō-hin** 骨董品(こっとうひん)

Aomori (prefecture) **Ao-mori-ken** 青森県(あおもりけん)

apple **ringo** りんご

appointment **yakusoku** 約束(やくそく)

are **dess** です

aren't **dewa arimasen** ではありません

aren't in **imasen** いません

around here **kono hen ni** このへんに

arrival time **tōchaku-jikan** 到着時間(とうちゃくじかん)

art museum **bijutsu-kan** 美術館(びじゅつかん)

as far as **made** まで

as far as Kyoto **Kyōto made** 京都(きょうと)まで

at Kyoto **Kyōto de** 京都(きょうと)で

at that corner **ano kado de** あの角(かど)で

at the end of **haji ni** 端(はじ)に

ATM card **kyasshu kādo** キャッシュカード

aunt (one's own aunt) **oba** おば

aunt (someone else's aunt) **oba-san** おばさん

Australia **Ōsutoraria** オーストラリア

Australian **Ōsutoraria-jin** オーストラリア人(じん)

autumn **aki** 秋(あき)

awhile **shibaraku** しばらく

B

bad weather **warui tenki** 悪(わる)い天気(てんき)

bag; baggage **nimotsu** 荷物(にもつ)

baggage checkroom **te-nimotsu ichiji azukari-jo** 手荷物(てにもつ)一時(いちじ)預り所(あずかりじょ)

bakery **pan-ya** パン屋(や)

bamboo shoot **takenoko** 竹(たけ)の子(こ)

bank **ginkō** 銀行(ぎんこう)

banquet **enkai** 宴会(えんかい)

baseball game **yakyū no shiai** 野球(やきゅう)の試合(しあい)

basement **chika** 地下(ちか)

bath (communal bath) **o-furo** お風呂(ふろ)

bathroom **basu-rūmu** バスルーム

beautiful **utsukushii** 美(うつく)しい

beef **gyū-niku** 牛肉(ぎゅうにく)

beer **biiru** ビール

before **mae; no mae (ni)** 前(まえ); の前(まえ)(に)

before a meal **shokuji no mae** 食事(しょくじ)の前(まえ)

behind **ushiro** 後(うし)ろ

better **motto ii** もっといい

big; big one **ōkii; ōkii-no** 大(おお)きい; 大(おお)きいの

bigger **motto ōkii** もっと大(おお)きい

bill **o-kanjo** お勘定(かんじょう)

birthday **tanjō-bi** 誕生日(たんじょうび)

bitter **nigai** 苦(にが)い

black tea **kōcha** 紅茶(こうちゃ)

blister **mame** マメ

bonito **katsuo** かつお

Bonsai (miniature potted tree or shrub) **bonsai** 盆栽(ぼんさい)

book **hon** 本(ほん)

bookstore **hon-ya** 本屋(ほんや)

botanical garden **shokubutsu-en** 植物園(しょくぶつえん)

bought **katta** 買(か)った

bound for **-yuki; -iki** 行(ゆ)き; 行(い)き

box lunch sold at stations or on trains **eki-ben** 駅弁(えきべん)

boy **otoko no ko** 男(おとこ)の子(こ)

break-up time **kaisan-jikan** 解散時間(かいさんじかん)

breakfast **asa-gohan** 朝(あさ)ごはん

bright **azayaka-na** 鮮(あざ)やかな

British person **Igirisu-jin** イギリス人(じん)

broiled eel and rice **una-don** うな丼(どん)

buckwheat noodles (dark and thin) **soba** そば

Buddhist temple **o-tera** お寺(てら)

building **biru** ビル

bullet train **Shinkansen** 新幹線(しんかんせん)

bun with bean-jam filling **o-manjū** おまんじゅう

bus; bus stop **basu; basu-tei** バス; バス停(てい)

buy **kaimahss** 買(か)います

buzzer (to get off) **buzā** ブザー

C

cabbage **kyabetsu** キャベツ

cake **kēki** ケーキ

calendar **karendā** カレンダー

camera **kamera** カメラ

camera shop **kamera-ya** カメラ屋(や)

camping **kyanpu** キャンプ

can be used **tsukaemahss** 使(つか)えます

can connect to **tsunagarimahss** つながります

Can I buy...? **... wo kaemahss ka?** …を買(か)えますか?

Can I rent...? **... wo kariraremahss ka?** …を借(か)りられますか?

Can I use...? **... tsukaemahss ka?** …使(つか)えますか?

can't connect **tsunagarimasen** つながりません

can't find **wakarimasen** わかりません

can't hear **kikoemasen** 聞(き)こえません

Canada **Kanada** カナダ

Canadian **Kanada-jin** カナダ人(じん)

cap **bōshi** 帽子(ぼうし)

car (number) **-gō-sha** 号車(ごうしゃ)

cardigan **kādegan** カーデガン

carrot **ninjin** にんじん

castle **o-shiro** お城(しろ)

cell phone **keitai-denwa; keitai** 携帯電話(けいたいでんわ); 携帯(けいたい)

Celsius **Sesshi** 摂氏(せっし)

charge **ryōkin** 料金(りょうきん)

cheap **yasui** 安(やす)い

check (bill) **o-kanjō** お勘定(かんじょう)

cherry blossom viewing **hanami; o-hanami** 花見(はなみ); お花見(はなみ)

Chiba (prefecture) **Chiba-ken** 千葉県(ちばけん)

chicken **tori-niku** 鶏肉(とりにく)

child **kodomo** 子(こ)ども

China **Chūgoku** 中国(ちゅうごく)

chinaware **tōjiki** 陶磁器(とうじき)

Chinese (language; person) **Chūgoku-go; Chūgoku-jin** 中国語(ちゅうごくご); 中国人(ちゅうごくじん)

Chinese cuisine **Chūgoku-ryōri; Chūka-ryōri** 中国料理(ちゅうごくりょうり); 中華料理(ちゅうかりょうり)

Chinese medicine **kanpō-yaku** 漢方薬(かんぽうやく)

chopsticks **o-hashi** お箸(はし)

Chuo Line (train line from Tokyo to Nagano Prefecture) **Chūō-sen** 中央線(ちゅうおうせん)

church **kyōkai** 教会(きょうかい)

city **machi** 町(まち)

climate **kikō** 気候(きこう)

clock **tokei** 時計(とけい)

closing hour of a store **heiten-jikan** 閉店時間(へいてんじかん)

cloth **ori-mono** 織物(おりもの)

cloth used to wrap things **furoshiki** 風呂敷(ふろしき)

cloudy **kumori** 曇(くも)り

coat **uwagi; kōto** 上着(うわぎ); コート

Coca-Cola **Koka-kōra** コカコーラ

cocktail party **kakuteru-pātii** カクテルパーティー

coffee **kōhii** コーヒー

coffee shop **kissa-ten** 喫茶店(きっさてん)

cold **kaze** 風邪(かぜ)

cold (temperature) **samui** 寒(さむ)い

cold (to the touch) **tsumetai** 冷(つめ)たい

cold medicine **kaze-gusuri** 風邪薬(かぜぐすり)

college **daigaku** 大学(だいがく)

company employee **kaisha-in** 会社員(かいしゃいん)

concert **konsāto** コンサート

conductor **shashō** 車掌(しゃしょう)

Congratulations. **Omedetō gozaimahss.** おめでとうございます。

connection **setsuzoku** 接続(せつぞく)

consulate **ryōji-kan** 領事館(りょうじかん)

convenience store **konbini** コンビニ

cooked rice **gohan** ごはん

cookie **kukkii** クッキー

cool **suzushii** 涼(すず)しい

corn **tōmorokoshi** とうもろこし

corner **kado** 角(かど)

corridor **rōka** 廊下(ろうか)

country **inaka** 田舎(いなか)

credit card **kurejitto-kādo** クレジットカード

cucumber **kyūri** きゅうり

cup **koppu** コップ

curry with rice **karē-raisu** カレーライス

cuttlefish **ika** イカ

D

daughter (one's own daughter or daughter-in-law) **musume** 娘(むすめ)

daughter (someone else's daughter or daughter-in-law) **musume-san** 娘(むすめ)さん

day after tomorrow **asatte** 明後日(あさって)

day before yesterday **ototoi** 一昨日(おととい)

day off **yasumi** 休み(やすみ)

day off from work **kyūka** 休暇(きゅうか)

deer **shika** 鹿(しか)

degree **do** 度(ど)

delicious **oishii** おいしい

department store **depāto** デパート

departure time **shuppatsu-jikan** 出発時間(しゅっぱつじかん)

diarrhea **geri** 下痢(げり)

did **shimashita** しました

different one **hoka-no** 他(ほか)の

dining car **shokudō-sha** 食堂車(しょくどうしゃ)

dining hall **shokudō** 食堂(しょくどう)

do **shimahss** します

doctor **isha** 医者(いしゃ)

don't go **ikimasen** 行(い)きません

don't have **arimasen** ありません

don't know **wakarimasen** わかりません

don't like **suki dewa arimasen** 好(す)きではありません

double room **daburu-rūmu** ダブルルーム

down **shita** 下(した)

dress (one-piece suit) **wan-piisu** ワンピース

drink **o-nomimono** お飲物(のみもの)

driver's license **unten menkyoshō** 運転免許証
(うんてんめんきょしょう)

E

early **hayaku** 早(はや)く

earthquake **jishin** 地震(じしん)

east **higashi** 東(ひがし)

egg **tamago** 玉子(たまご)

eggplant **nasu** なす

Ehime (prefecture) **Ehime-ken** 愛媛県(えひめけん)

electrical goods **denka-seihin** 電化製品(でんかせいひん)

elevator **erebētā** エレベーター

embassy **taishi-kan** 大使館(たいしかん)

engagement **yakusoku** 約束(やくそく)

English **Ei-go** 英語(えいご)

English-speaking doctor **Ei-go wo hanasu isha** 英語(えいご)を話(はな)す医者(いしゃ)

entrance **iriguchi** 入口(いりぐち)

entrance to board **nori-ba** 乗(の)り場(ば)

escalator **esukarētā** エスカレーター

every month **mai-tsuki; mai-getsu** 毎月(まいつき; まいげつ)

every night **mai-ban** 毎晩(まいばん)

every week **mai-shū** 毎週(まいしゅう)

every year **mai-nen; mai-toshi** 毎年(まいねん; まいとし)

every day **mai-nichi** 毎日(まいにち)

excursion boat **yūran-sen** 遊覧船(ゆうらんせん)

Excuse me. **Sumimasen.** すみません。

exhibition **tenran-kai** 展覧会(てんらんかい)

exit **deguchi** 出口(でぐち)

expensive **takai** 高(たか)い

exposition **hakuran-kai** 博覧会(はくらんかい)

express **kyūkō** 急行(きゅうこう)

expressway **kōsoku-dōro** 高速道路(こうそくどうろ)

extension **naisen** 内線(ないせん)

extra large (for clothes) **eru-eru; ekkusu-eru** LL(エルエル); XL(エックスエル)

F

Fahrenheit **Kashi** 華氏(かし)

fall (rain, snow) **furimahss** 降(ふ)ります

famous **yūmei na** 有名(ゆうめい)な

far **tōi** 遠(とお)い

fare table **unchin-hyō** 運賃表(うんちんひょう)

farewell party **sōbetsu-kai** 送別会(そうべつかい)

fast food restaurant **fasuto fūdo ten** ファストフード店(てん)

father (one's own father) **chichi** 父(ちち)

father (someone else's father; also used when addressing one's own father) **otō-san** お父(とう)さん

female **onna** 女(おんな)

ferry **ferii** フェリー

festival **o-matsuri** お祭(まつ)り

fever **netsu** 熱(ねつ)

field trip **kengaku-ryokō** 見学旅行(けんがくりょこう)

fine **genki** 元気(げんき)

fine weather **hare** 晴(は)れ

fireworks **hanabi** 花火(はなび)

fireworks display **hanabi-taikai** 花火大会(はなびたいかい)

fish **sakana** 魚(さかな)

flashy; gaudy **hade-na** 派手(はで)な

flatfish **hirame** ひらめ

floor **kai** 階(かい)

fog **kiri** 霧(きり)

folding fan **sensu** 扇子(せんす)

folk-art handicraft **mingei-hin** 民芸品(みんげいひん)

foot **ashi** 足(あし)

for free **muryō de** 無料(むりょう)で

fork **fōku** フォーク

France **Furansu** フランス

French (language; person) **Furansu-go; Furansu-jin** フランス語(ご); フランス人(じん)

fresh **atarashii** 新(あたら)しい

Friday **Kin-yōbi** 金曜日(きんようび)

friend **tomodachi** 友(とも)だち

front desk **furonto** フロント

fruit **kudamono; furūtsu** 果物(くだもの); フルーツ

Fukui (prefecture) **Fukui-ken** 福井県(ふくいけん)

Fukuoka (prefecture) **Fukuoka-ken** 福岡県(ふくおかけん)

Fukushima (prefecture) **Fukushima-ken** 福島県(ふくしまけん)

full **ippai; manseki** 一杯(いっぱい); 満席(まんせき)

funeral **o-sōshiki** お葬式(そうしき)

G

gallery **garō** 画廊(がろう)

game **shiai** 試合(しあい)

garden **niwa** 庭(にわ)

gas station **gasorin-sutando** ガソリンスタンド

German (language; person) **Doitsu-go; Doitsu-jin** ドイツ語(ご); ドイツ人(じん)

Germany **Doitsu** ドイツ

gift shop **gifuto-shoppu** ギフトショップ

gift-wrap **okuri-mono yō ni tsutsumu** 贈(おく)り物(もの)用(よう)に包(つつ)む

Gifu (prefecture) **Gifu-ken** 岐阜県(ぎふけん)

Ginza **Ginza** 銀座(ぎんざ)

girl **onna no ko** 女(おんな)の子(こ)

Glad to meet you, too. **Kochira koso (yoroshiku).** こちらこそ(よろしく)。

Glad to meet you. **Dōzo yoroshiku.** どうぞよろしく。

glass **koppu** コップ

gloves **tebukuro** 手袋(てぶくろ)

go **ikimahss** 行(い)きます

go (board game played with black and white stones) **go** 碁(ご)

go out **dekakemahss** 出(で)かけます

golf tournament **gorufu no konpe** ゴルフのコンペ

good **ii** いい

Good afternoon. **Konnichi-wa.** こんにちは。

Good evening. **Konbanwa.** こんばんは。

Good morning. **Ohayō gozaimahss.** おはようございます。

Good night. **Oyasumi-nasai.** おやすみなさい。

Goodbye. **Sayōnara.** さようなら。

grandchild (one's own grandchild) **mago** 孫(まご)

grandchild (someone else's grandchild) **o-mago-san** お孫(まご)さん

grape **budō** ぶどう

Great Britain, the United Kingdom **Igirisu** イギリス

green light **ao-shingō** 青信号(あおしんごう)

green tea **o-cha** お茶(ちゃ)

grilled, skewered chicken **yakitori** 焼(や)き鳥(とり)

group tour **dantai-ryokō** 団体旅行(だんたいりょこう)

guidebook **gaido-bukku** ガイドブック

Gunma (prefecture) **Gunma-ken** 群馬県(ぐんまけん)

H

half (past) **han** 半(はん)

hall **rōka** 廊下(ろうか)

hand **te** 手(て)

hanging picture; hanging scroll **kake-mono** 掛(か)け物(もの)

hard **katai** 固(かた)い

hat **bōshi** 帽子(ぼうし)

have this laundered **kore wo sentaku shitemorau** これを洗濯(せんたく)してもらう

he **kare** 彼(かれ)

head **atama** 頭(あたま)

healthy **genki** 元気(げんき)

heater **danbō; hiitā** 暖房(だんぼう); ヒーター

heavy **omoi** 重(おも)い

Hello. **Konnichiwa.** こんにちは。

Hello. (on the telephone) **Moshi-moshi.** もしもし。

Help! **Tasukete!** 助(たす)けて!

here **koko; koko de; koko wa** ここ; ここで; ここは

hiking **haikingu** ハイキング

Himeji Castle **Himeji-jō** 姫路城(ひめじじょう)

Hiroshima **Hiroshima** 広島(ひろしま)

Hiroshima (prefecture) **Hiroshima-ken** 広島県(ひろしまけん)

historical site **shiseki** 史跡(しせき)

Hokkaido (prefecture) **Hokkaidō** 北海道(ほっかいどう)

holiday **yasumi** 休みや(す)み

horse mackerel **iwashi** いわし

hospital **byōin** 病院(びょういん)

hot **atsui** 熱(あつ)い

hot day **atsui hi** 暑(あつ)い日(ひ)

hot or cold hand towel used to wipe one's hands before eating **o-shibori** おしぼり

hot spring **onsen** 温泉(おんせん)

hotel **hoteru** ホテル

how **dō; dō-yatte** どう; どうやって

how about **ikaga; dō** いかが; どう

How are you? **O-genki dess ka?** お元気(げんき)ですか?

How do you do? **Hajime-mashite.** はじめまして。

how many **ikutsu** いくつ

how many people **nan-mei-sama** 何名様(なんめいさま)

how much **ikura** いくら

How much is it? **Ikura dess ka?** いくらですか?

humid **mushi-atsui** 蒸(む)し暑(あつ)い

hungry **suite imahss** 空(す)いています

hurt **itai** 痛(いた)い

husband (one's husband) **otto** 夫(おっと)

husband (someone else's husband) **danna-san** だんなさん

Hyogo (prefecture) **Hyōgo-ken** 兵庫県(ひょうごけん)

I

I **watashi** 私(わたし)

I don't understand. **Wakari-masen.** わかりません。

I have many bags. **Nimotsu ga takusan arimahss.** 荷物(にもつ)がたくさんあります。

I understand. **Wakari-mahss.** わかります。

I'm full. **O-naka ga ippai dess.** お腹(なか)が一杯(いっぱい)です。

I'm poor at... **...heta dess** …へたです

Ibaraki (prefecture) **Ibara-ki-ken** 茨城県(いばらきけん)

ice **kōri** 氷(こおり)

ice cream **aisu-kuriimu** アイスクリーム

ID card **mibun shōmeisho; aidii kādo** 身分証明書(みぶんしょうめいしょ); アイディーカード

Imperial Hotel **Teikoku Hoteru** 帝国(ていこく)ホテル

in **naka** 中(なか)

in English **Ei-go de** 英語(えいご)で

in front **mae** 前(まえ)

in Japanese **Nihon-go de** 日本語(にほんご)で

in Kyoto **Kyōto de** 京都(きょうと)で

in Nara **Nara de** 奈良(なら)で

in the middle of **chūō ni** 中央(ちゅうおう)に

in this vicinity **kono hen ni** このへんに

in trouble **komatte** 困(こま)って

in your room **o-heya de** お部屋(へや)で

Indonesian (language; person) **Indoneshia-go; Indoneshia-jin** インドネシア語(ご); インドネシア人(じん)

inexpensive **yasui** 安(やす)い

inexpensive one **yasui-no** 安(やす)いの

information office **annai-jo** 案内所(あんないじょ)

injection **chūsha** 注射(ちゅうしゃ)

injury **kega** けが

Inland Sea **Seto-naikai** 瀬戸内海(せとないかい)

inside **naka** 中(なか)

international telephone call **kokusai-denwa** 国際電話(こくさいでんわ)

Internet café; cyber café; manga café **Intānetto kafe; manga kissa** インターネットカフェ; 漫画喫茶(まんがきっさ)

intersection **kōsaten** 交差点(こうさてん)

is **dess** です

Ise Shrine **Ise Jingū** 伊勢神宮(いせじんぐう)

Ishikawa (prefecture) **Ishikawa-ken** 石川県(いしかわけん)

isn't **dewa arimasen** ではありません

isn't in **imasen** いません

Isn't it? **Ne?** ね？

It was delicious. **Oishikatta dess.** おいしかったです。

It'll probably... **tabun... desho** たぶん…でしょう

It's delicious. **Oishii dess.** おいしいです。

It's my treat. **Watashi no ogori dess.** 私(わたし)の おごりです。

Italian (language; person) **Itaria-go; Itaria-jin** イタリア語(ご); イタリア 人(じん)

Italy **Itaria** イタリア

Iwate (prefecture) **Iwate-ken** 岩手県(いわてけん)

Izumo Shrine **Izumo Taisha** 出雲大社(いずもた いしゃ)

J

jacket **uwagi** 上着(うわぎ)

Japanese (language; person) **Nihon-go; Nihon-jin** 日本語(にほんご); 日本人 (にほんじん)

Japanese cuisine **Nihon-ryōri** 日本料理(にほんり ょうり)

Japanese doll **Nihon ningyō** 日本人形(にほん にんぎょう)

Japanese inn **ryokan** 旅館 (りょかん)

journalist **kisha** 記者(きしゃ)

JR Pass **Jei Āru Pass** ジェ イアールパス

K

Kabuki **Kabuki** 歌舞伎 (かぶき)

Kabuki Theater **Kabukiza** 歌舞伎座(かぶきざ)

Kagawa (prefecture) **Kaga-wa-ken** 香川県(かがわ けん)

Kagoshima (prefecture) **Kagoshima-ken** 鹿児島 県(かごしまけん)

Kanagawa (prefecture) **Kanagawa-ken** 神奈川県 (かながわけん)

Kanda (place name in Tokyo) **Kanda** 神田(かんだ)

key **kagi** 鍵(かぎ)

kimono **kimono** 着物(き もの)

kiosk **kiosuku** キヨスク

Kiyomizudera Temple (lit., Pure Water Temple) **Kiyo-mizu-dera** 清水寺(きよみ ずでら)

Kochi (prefecture) **Kōchi-ken** 高知県(こうちけん)

Korea (ROK) **Kankoku** 韓国(かんこく)

Korean (language; person) **Kankoku-go; Kankoku-jin** 韓国語(かんこくご); 韓国人(かんこくじん)

Kumamoto (prefecture) **Kumamoto-ken** 熊本県 (くまもとけん)

Kyoto **Kyōto** 京都(きょうと)

Kyoto (prefecture) **Kyōto-fu** 京都府(きょうとふ)

L

lacquerware **nuri-mono** 塗(ぬ)り物(もの)

lake **mizuumi** 湖(みず うみ)

landing **nori-ba** 乗(の)り 場(ば)

lantern **chōchin** 提灯(ちょ うちん)

laptop **rappu toppu** ラッ プトップ

large (for clothes) **eru** L(エル)

large statue of Buddha **daibutsu** 大仏(だいぶつ)

last month **sengetsu** 先月 (せんげつ)

last week **senshū** 先週(せ んしゅう)

last year **kyonen** 去年(き
ょねん)
late **osoku** 遅(おそ)く
lawyer **bengo-shi** 弁護士
(べんごし)
leave **dekakemahss** 出(で)
かけます
left **hidari** 左(ひだり)
leg **ashi** 脚(あし)
letter **tegami** 手紙(てがみ)
lettuce **retasu** レタス
library **tosho-kan** 図書館
(としょかん)
light **karui** 軽(かる)い
light cotton kimono **yukata**
浴衣(ゆかた)
lightning **inazuma** 稲妻
(いなずま)
like **suki** 好(す)き
Limited Express **Tokkyū**
特急(とっきゅう)
line (train) **-sen** 線(せん)
listen **kiku; kikimahss**
聞(き)く;聞(き)きます
lobby **robii** ロビー
local telephone call
shinai-denwa 市内電話
(しないでんわ)
local train **futsū** 普通(ふ
つう)
locker **rokkā** ロッカー

long distance telephone call
chōkyori-denwa 長距離
電話(ちょうきょりでんわ)
lost **nakushmashita** なく
しました
lost (the way) **mayoimashita** 迷(まよ)いました
lotus root **renkon** レンコン
lunch **hiru-gohan** 昼(ひる)
ごはん

M

mackerel **saba** さば
magazine **zasshi** 雑誌(ざ
っし)
mahjong **mājan** 麻雀(まー
じゃん)
mail **yūbin** 郵便(ゆうびん)
make a telephone call **o-
denwa shimahss** お電話
(でんわ)します
male **otoko** 男(おとこ)
man **otoko no hito** 男(おと
こ)の人(ひと)
manga; comic café **manga
kissa** 漫画喫茶(まんが
きっさ)
many **takusan** たくさん
map **chizu** 地図(ちず)
match **shiai** 試合(しあい)
meal **gohan; shokuji** ごは
ん;食事(しょくじ)

meat **niku** 肉(にく)
medicine **kusuri** 薬(くすり)
medium (for clothes) **emu**
M(エム)
meeting time **shūgō-jikan**
集合時間(しゅうごうじかん)
Meiji Shrine **Meiji-Jingu**
明治神宮(めいじじんぐう)
melon **meron** メロン
message **messēji** メッセ
ージ
Mie (prefecture) **Mie-ken**
三重県(みえけん)
milk **gyū-nyū** 牛乳(ぎゅう
にゅう)
miso (bean paste) **miso**
味噌(みそ)
Miyagi (prefecture) **Mi-
yagi-ken** 宮城県(みやぎ
けん)
Miyazaki (prefecture) **Miyazaki-ken** 宮崎県(みや
ざきけん)
Monday **Getsu-yōbi** 月曜
日(げつようび)
money **o-kane** お金(かね)
monument **kinen-hi** 記念
碑(きねんひ)
more **motto** もっと
mother (one's own mother
or mother-in-law) **haha**
母(はは)

mother (someone else's mother or mother-in-law) **okā-san** お母(かあ)さん

Mount Fuji **Fujisan** 富士山(ふじさん)

Mount Sakurajima **Sakurajima** 桜島(さくらじま)

mountain **yama** 山(やま)

mountain climbing **yamanobori** 山登(やまのぼ)り

movie **eiga** 映画(えいが)

movie theater **eiga-kan** 映画館(えいがかん)

Mr.; Mrs.; Ms.; Miss Tanaka **Tanaka-san** 田中(たなか)さん

Mr.; Mrs.; Ms.; Miss Tanaka's **Tanaka-san no** 田中(たなか)さんの

museum **hakubutsu-kan** 博物館(はくぶつかん)

my **watashi no** 私(わたし)の

N

Nagano (prefecture) **Nagano-ken** 長野県(ながのけん)

Nagasaki (prefecture) **Nagasaki-ken** 長崎県(ながさきけん)

name **namae** 名前(なまえ)

napkin **napukin** ナプキン

Nara **Nara** 奈良(なら)

Nara (prefecture) **Nara-ken** 奈良県(ならけん)

national holiday **saijitsu** 祭日(さいじつ)

near **chikai; soba** 近(ちか)い; そば

new **atarashii** 新(あたら)しい

newspaper **shinbun** 新聞(しんぶん)

newspaper stand **shinbun uriba** 新聞(しんぶん)売(う)り場(ば)

next day **tsugi no hi** 次(つぎ)の日(ひ)

next month **raigetsu** 来月(らいげつ)

next week **raishū** 来週(らいしゅう)

next year **rainen** 来年(らいねん)

nice **ii** いい

Niigata (prefecture) **Niigata-ken** 新潟県(にいがたけん)

Nijo Castle **Nijō-jō** 二条城(にじょうじょう)

no **iie** いいえ

no charge **muryō** 無料(むりょう)

no vacancy **manseki** 満席(まんせき)

No, I don't understand. **Iie, wakarimasen.** いいえ、わかりません。

No, I'm not. **Chigaimahss.** 違(ちが)います。

No, thank you. **Iie, kekkō dess.** いいえ、けっこうです。

non-reserved seat **jiyū-seki** 自由席(じゆうせき)

non-smoking car **kin'en-sha** 禁煙車(きんえんしゃ)

noodles (white and fat) **udon** うどん

north **kita** 北(きた)

not tasty **oishiku nai** おいしくない

not work very well **chōshi ga yokunai** 調子(ちょうし)がよくない

now **ima** 今(いま)

nurse **kango-fu** 看護婦(かんごふ)

O

ocean **umi** 海(うみ)

octopus **tako** タコ

of no **no** の

Oita (prefecture) **Ōita-ken** 大分県(おおいたけん)

Okayama (prefecture) **Okayama-ken** 岡山県(おかやまけん)

Okinawa (prefecture) **Okinawa-ken** 沖縄県(おきなわけん)

old **furui** 古(ふる)い

older brother (one's own older brother or brother-in-law) **ani** 兄(あに)

older brother (someone else's older brother or brother-in-law) **onii-san** お兄(にい)さん

older sister (one's own older sister or sister-in-law) **ane** 姉(あね)

older sister (someone else's older sister or sister-in-law) **onē-san** お姉(ねえ)さん

on Saturday **Do-yōbi ni** 土曜日(どようび)に

on the map **chizu de** 地図(ちず)で

on the train **densha ni** 電車(でんしゃ)に

on what day of the week **nan-yōbi ni** 何曜日(なんようび)に

once more **mō ichido** もう一度(いちど)

one of these **kore wo hitotsu; kono uchi no hitotsu** これを１つ(ひとつ); このうちのひとつ

one of these days **chikai uchi ni** 近(ちか)いうちに

one-way (ticket) **katamichi (-kippu)** 片道(かたみち)(切符(きっぷ))

onion **tamanegi** 玉(たま)ねぎ

open field **heiya** 平野(へいや)

opening hour of a store **kaiten-jikan** 開店時間(かいてんじかん)

operator **kōkan-shu** 交換手(こうかんしゅ)

orange **orenji** オレンジ

orange juice **orenji-jūsu** オレンジジュース

Osaka **Ōsaka** 大阪(おおさか)

Osaka (prefecture) **Ōsaka-fu** 大阪府(おおさかふ)

outside **soto** 外(そと)

over there **asoko** あそこ

overseas travel **kaigai-ryokō** 海外旅行(かいがいりょこう)

oyster bed (cultivated) **kaki-yōshokujō** 牡蠣養殖場(かきようしょくじょう)

P

p.m. **gogo** 午後(ごご)

pagoda **tō** 塔(とう)

painting **e** 絵(え)

pants (trousers) **pantsu** パンツ

park **kōen** 公園(こうえん)

parking lot **chūsha-jō** 駐車場(ちゅうしゃじょう)

party **pātii** パーティー

passport **pasupōto** パスポート

peach **momo** 桃(もも)

pear **nashi** 梨(なし)

pearl **shinju** 真珠(しんじゅ)

persimmon **kaki** 柿(かき)

person **hito** 人(ひと)

person who speaks **hanasu hito** 話(はな)す人(ひと)

personal computer **paso-kon** パソコン

pharmacy **kusuri-ya; yak-kyoku** 薬屋(くすりや); 薬局(やっきょく)

photo; photograph; picture **shashin** 写真(しゃしん)

photo of deer **shika no shashin** 鹿(しか)の写真(しゃしん)

physical exercise **undō** 運動(うんどう)

pickle **tsuke-mono** 漬(つ)け物(もの)

pickpocket **suri** すり

picnic **pikunikku** ピクニック

place of interest (tourist attractions) **meisho** 名所(めいしょ)

plain **heiya** 平野(へいや)

plate **sara** 皿(さら)

platform **hōmu; puratto hōmu** ホーム; プラットホーム

please **kudasai; o-negai shimahss** ください; お願(ねが)いします

please (do something) **dōzo** どうぞ

please break (into change) **kuzushite kudasai** くずしてください

please call **yonde kudasai** 呼(よ)んでください

please give **kudasai** ください

please go **itte kudasai** 行(い)ってください

Please let me out. **Oroshite kudasai.** 降(お)ろしてください。

please say **itte kudasai** 言(い)ってください

Please say it once more. **Mō ichido itte kudasai.** もう一度(いちど)、言(い)ってください。

please send **okutte kudasai** 送(おく)ってください

please show **misete kudasai** 見(み)せてください

please speak **hanashite kudasai** 話(はな)してください

Please speak in English. **Ei-go de hanashite kudasai.** 英語(えいご)で話(はな)してください。

Please speak slowly. **Yukkuri hanashite kudasai.** ゆっくり話(はな)してください。

please stop (a car) **tomete kudasai** 止(と)めてください

please take **totte kudasai** 撮(と)ってください

please tell **oshiete kudasai** 教(おし)えてください

please turn **magatte kudasai** 曲(ま)がってください

please wait **o-machi kudasai; matte kudasai** お待(ま)ちください; 待(ま)ってください

please wrap **tsutsunde kudasai** 包(つつ)んでください

please write **kaite kudasai** 書(か)いてください

pocket Wi-Fi router **poketto Waifai** ポケットWi-Fi (ワイファイ)

police box **kōban** 交番(こうばん)

police station **keisatsu-sho** 警察署(けいさつしょ)

popular dish of meat, vegetable, bean curd, etc. **suki-yaki** すき焼(や)き

pork **buta-niku** 豚肉(ぶたにく)

pork cutlet **tonkatsu** とんかつ

porter **akabō** 赤帽(あかぼう)

Portugal **Porutogaru** ポルトガル

Portuguese (language; person) **Porutogaru-go; Porutogaru-jin** ポルトガル語(ご); ポルトガル人(じん)

post office **yūbin-kyoku** 郵便局(ゆうびんきょく)

postcard **e-hagaki** 絵葉書(えはがき)

potato **jagaimo** じゃがいも

pottery **seto-mono** 瀬戸物(せともの)

prefecture **ken** 県(けん)

prepaid cell phone **puri peido keitai** プリペイド携帯(けいたい)

pretty **kirei-na** きれいな

previous day **mae no hi** 前(まえ)の日(ひ)

price **nedan** 値段(ねだん)

probably **tabun** たぶん

promise **yakusoku** 約束(やくそく)

public square **hiro-ba** 広場(ひろば)

public telephone **kōshū-denwa** 公衆電話(こうしゅうでんわ)

pumpkin **kabocha** かぼちゃ

R

radio **rajio** ラジオ

rain; rainy **ame** 雨(あめ)

raincoat **reinkōto** レインコート

rapid train **kaisoku** 快速(かいそく)

raw **nama** 生(なま)

read **yomu; yomimahss** 読(よ)む; 読(よ)みます

receipt **ryōshū-sho** 領収書(りょうしゅうしょ)

reception **uketsuke** 受付(うけつけ)

reception desk **furonto** フロント

red light **aka-shingō** 赤信号(あかしんごう)

refined **jimi-na** 地味(じみ)な

regional specialty **meisan** 名産(めいさん)

reporter **kisha** 記者(きしゃ)

reservation **yoyaku** 予約(よやく)

reserved seat **shitei-seki** 指定席(していせき)

reserved-seat ticket **zaseki shitei-ken** 座席指定券(ざせきしていけん)

restaurant **resutoran** レストラン

restroom **o-tearai** お手洗(てあらい)

return **kaeru** 帰(かえ)る; 帰(かえ)ります

rice bowl **chawan** 茶碗(ちゃわん)

rice cracker **senbei** せんべい

rice paddy **suiden** 水田(すいでん)

right **migi** 右(みぎ)

right away **sugu** すぐ

river **kawa** 川(かわ)

road **dōro; michi** 道路(どうろ); 道(みち)

roof **okujō** 屋上(おくじょう)

room **heya** 部屋(へや)

room with a bathroom **basu-tsuki no heya** バス付(つ)きの部屋(へや)

Roppongi **Roppongi** 六本木(ろっぽんぎ)

round **marui** 丸(まる)い

round-trip (ticket) **ōfuku (-kippu)** 往復(おうふく)(切符(きっぷ))

rural area **inaka** 田舎(いなか)

Russia **Roshia** ロシア

Russian (language; person) **Roshia-go; Roshia-jin** ロシア語(ご); ロシア人(じん)

S

Saga (prefecture) **Saga-ken** 佐賀県(さがけん)

Saitama (prefecture) **Saitama-ken** 埼玉県(さいたまけん)

saké (Japanese rice wine) **o-sake** お酒(さけ)

saké bottle **tokkuri** 徳利(とっくり)

saké cup **sakazuki** 杯(さかずき)

salad **sarada** サラダ

salmon **sake** さけ

salmon roe **ikura** イクラ

salty **shoppai** 塩(しょ)っぱい

sandwich **sandoitchi** サンドイッチ

sardine **iwashi** いわし

Saturday **Do-yōbi** 土曜日(どようび)

saw **mimashita** 見(み)ました

sculpture **chōkoku** 彫刻(ちょうこく)

sea urchin **uni** うに

season **kisetsu** 季節(きせつ)

seaweed **nori** 海苔(のり)

secretary **hisho** 秘書(ひしょ)

see **mimahss** 見(み)ます

See you later. **Dewa mata.** では、また。

Sensoji Temple **Sensōji** 浅草寺(せんそうじ)

service **sābiss** サービス

service charge **sābisu-ryō** サービス料(りょう)

set meal (includes main dish, soup, pickles, and rice) **teishoku** 定食(ていしょく)

she **kanojo** 彼女(かのじょ)

Shiga (prefecture) **Shiga-ken** 滋賀県(しがけん)

shiitake mushroom **shiitake** しいたけ

Shimane (prefecture) **Shimane-ken** 島根県(しまねけん)

Shinjuku **Shinjuku** 新宿(しんじゅく)

Shinjuku Gyoen National Garden **Shinjuku Gyoen** 新宿(しんじゅく)御苑(ぎょえん)

Shinto shrine **Jinja** 神社(じんじゃ)

Shinto shrine archway **Torii** 鳥居(とりい)

ship **fune** 船(ふね)

shirt **shatsu** シャツ

Shizuoka (prefecture) **Shizuoka-ken** 静岡県(しずおかけん)

shochu (distilled spirit usually drunk with water or a mixer) **shōchū** 焼酎(しょうちゅう)

shortly **mō sugu** もうすぐ

shot **chūsha** 注射(ちゅうしゃ)

Should I go? **Ikeba ii dess ka?** 行(い)けばいいですか?

shower **niwaka-ame** にわか雨(あめ)

shrimp **ebi** エビ

sick **guai ga warui** 具合(ぐあい)が悪(わる)い

sightseeing **kankō** 観光(かんこう)

silk **kinu** 絹(きぬ)

SIM card **shimu kādo** SIM(シム)カード

single room **shinguru-rūmu** シングルルーム

skirt **sukāto** スカート

skyscraper **kōsō-biru** 高層(こうそう)ビル

slowly **yukkuri** ゆっくり

small **chiisai** 小(ちい)さい

small (for clothes) **esu** S(エス)

snow **yuki** 雪(ゆき)

sock(s) **kutsushita** 靴下(くつした)

soft **yawarakai** 柔(やわ)らかい

some more **motto** もっと

son (one's own son or son-in-law) **musuko** 息子(むすこ)

son (someone else's son or son-in-law) **musuko-san** 息子(むすこ)さん

soon **mō sugu** もうすぐ

Sorry, but... **Sumimasen ga...** すみませんが…

soup **o-sui-mono** お吸(す)い物(もの)

sour **suppai** 酸(す)っぱい

south **minami** 南(みなみ)

souvenir **o-miyage** お土産(みやげ)

Spain **Supein** スペイン

Spanish (language; person) **Supein-go; Supein-jin** スペイン語(ご); スペイン人(じん)

spicy **karai** 辛(から)い

spoon **supūn** スプーン

sports **supōtsu** スポーツ

spot **supotto** スポット

spring **haru** 春(はる)

square **shikakui** 四角(しかく)い

squid **ika** いか

stadium **sutajiamu** スタジアム

stairs **kaidan** 階段(かいだん)

stale **furui** 古(ふる)い

stamp **kitte** 切手(きって)

start **hajimarimahss** 始(はじ)まります

station **eki** 駅(えき)

station employee **eki-in** 駅員(えきいん)

station shop **eki no baiten** 駅(えき)の売店(ばいてん)

statue **zō** 像(ぞう)

statue of a Buddha **butsuzō** 仏像(ぶつぞう)

stole **nusumimashita** 盗(ぬす)みみました

stomach **o-naka** お腹(なか)

stop at **ni tomarimahss** に止(と)まります

store **mise** 店(みせ)

storm **arashi** 嵐(あらし)

straight ahead **koko wo massugu** ここをまっすぐ

street **michi** 道(みち)

student **gakusei** 学生(がくせい)

subdued **jimi-na** 地味(じみ)な

subway **chika-tetsu** 地下鉄(ちかてつ)

subway station **chika-tetsu no eki** 地下鉄(ちかてつ)の駅(えき)

summer **natsu** 夏(なつ)

summer vacation **natsu-ya-sumi** 夏休(なつやす)み

Sunday **Nichi-yōbi** 日曜日(にちようび)

supper **ban-gohan** 晩(ばん)ごはん

sushi **o-sushi** お寿司(すし)

sweatshirt **torēnā; suetto** トレーナー; スエット

sweater **sēta** セーター

sweet **amai** 甘(あま)い

sweets **o-kashi** お菓子(かし)

swollen **harete imahss** 腫(は)れています

T

T-shirt **tii-shatsu** T(ティー)シャツ

tablet **taburetto** タブレット

take **torimahss** 撮(と)ります

tangerine **mikan** みかん

taste **aji** 味(あじ)

tax **zeikin** 税金(ぜいきん)

taxi **takushii** タクシー

taxi stand **takushii-noriba** タクシー乗(の)り場(ば)

tea field **cha-batake** 茶畑(ちゃばたけ)

teacher **sensei** 先生(せんせい)

teacup **yu-nomi** 湯(ゆ)のみ

teatime **o-cha no jikan** お茶(ちゃ)の時間(じかん)

telephone **denwa** 電話(でんわ)

telephone bill **denwa-ryōkin** 電話料金(でんわりょうきん)

telephone card **terefon-kādo** テレフォンカード

telephone directory **denwa-chō** 電話帳(でんわちょう)

telephone number **denwa-bangō** 電話番号(でんわばんごう)

television **terebi** テレビ

temperature **ondo** 温度(おんど)

temple gate **sanmon** 山門(さんもん)

tempura (deep-fried food) **tenpura** 天(てん)ぷら

tender **yawarakai** 柔(やわ)らかい

textile **ori-mono** 織物(おりもの)

Thai (language; person) **Tai-go; Tai-jin** タイ語(ご); タイ人(じん)

Thank you. **Dōmo arigatō.; Arigatō.** どうもありがとう。; ありがとう。

Thank you. (It was delicious.) **Gochisō-sama deshita.** ごちそうさまでした。

that **are; ano** あれ; あの

that one **are** あれ

that person **ano hito** あの人(ひと)

that place **asoko** あそこ

That's right. **Sō dess.** そうです。

the day after tomorrow **asatte** 明後日(あさって)

the Golden Pavilion **Kinkaku-ji** 金閣寺(きんかくじ)

the Imperial Palace **Kōkyo** 皇居(こうきょ)

the Internet **Intānetto** インターネット

the Kabuki Theater **Kabuki-za** 歌舞伎座(かぶきざ)

the Pacific Ocean **Taihei-yō** 太平洋(たいへいよう)

the Sea of Japan **Nihon-kai** 日本海(にほんかい)

the Silver Pavilion **Ginkaku-ji** 銀閣寺(ぎんかくじ)

the time a group disperses **kaisan-jikan** 解散時間(かいさんじかん)

the time a performance starts **kaien-jikan** 開演時間(かいえんじかん)

The United States **Amerika** アメリカ

theater **gekijō** 劇場(げきじょう)

there are; there is **arimahss** あります

thermometer **taion-kei** 体温計(たいおんけい)

thief **dorobō** 泥棒(どろぼう)

this **kore; kono** これ; この

this evening **konban** 今晩(こんばん)

this month **kongetsu** 今月(こんげつ)

this place **koko** ここ

this train **kono densha** この電車(でんしゃ)

this watch **kono tokei** この時計(とけい)

this week **konshū** 今週(こんしゅう)

this year **kotoshi** 今年(ことし)

thunder **kaminari** 雷(かみなり)

Thursday **Moku-yōbi** 木曜日(もくようび)

ticket **kippu** 切符(きっぷ)

ticket gate **kaisatsu-guchi** 改札口(かいさつぐち)

ticket machine **(kippu no) jidō-hanbaiki** (切符(きっぷ)の)自動販売機(じどうはんばいき)

time set for an appointment **yakusoku no jikan** 約束(やくそく)の時間(じかん)

timetable **jikoku-hyō** 時刻表(じこくひょう)

to **made; e** まで; へ

to the left **hidari e** 左(ひだり)へ

to the park **kōen made** 公園(こうえん)まで

to the right **migi e** 右(みぎ)へ

Tochigi (prefecture) **Tochigi-ken** 栃木県(とちぎけん)

Todaiji Temple **Tōdai-ji** 東大寺(とうだいじ)

today **kyō** 今日(きょう)

tofu **tōfu** 豆腐(とうふ)

Toji Temple **Tō-ji** 東寺(とうじ)

Tokushima (prefecture) **Tokushima-ken** 徳島県(とくしまけん)

Tokyo (prefecture) **Tōkyō-to** 東京都(とうきょうと)

Tokyo Disneyland **Tōkyō Dizunii rando** 東京(とうきょう)ディズニーランド

Tokyo Sky Tree **Tōkyō Sukai Tsurii** 東京(とうきょう)スカイツリー

Tokyo Station **Tōkyō-eki** 東京駅(とうきょうえき)

Tokyo Tower **Tōkyō Tawā** 東京(とうきょう)タワー

tomato **tomato** トマト

tomorrow **ashita** 明日(あした)

tomorrow morning **ashita no asa** 明日(あした)の朝(あさ)

tonight **konban** 今晩(こんばん)

took **torimashita** 撮(と)りました

tooth **ha** 歯(は)

Toshogu Shrine **Nikkō Tōshōgū** 日光東照宮(にっこうとうしょうぐう)

Tottori (prefecture) **Tottori-ken** 鳥取県(とっとりけん)

tough **katai** 固(かた)い

tour bus **kankō-basu** 観光(かんこう)バス

tour of **meguri** めぐり

tour of a city **shinai-kankō** 市内観光(しないかんこう)

tour of a factory, institution, etc. **kengaku-ryokō** 見学旅行(けんがくりょこう)

tour of Kyushu **Kyūshū-meguri** 九州(きゅうしゅう)めぐり

tower **tō** 塔(とう)

town **machi** 町(まち)

Toyama (prefecture) **Toyama-ken** 富山県(とやまけん)

track (number)... **...ban-sen** …番線(ばんせん)

traditional **dentō-teki-na** 伝統的(でんとうてき)な

traditional Japanese wrestling (sumo) **sumō** 相撲(すもう)

traditional, handmade paper **washi** 和紙(わし)

traffic light **shingō** 信号(しんごう)

train **densha** 電車(でんしゃ)

train station **eki** 駅(えき)

transfer **nori-kae** 乗(の)り換(か)え

travel bureau **ryokō-sentā** 旅行(りょこう)センター

travel insurance **ryokō-hoken** 旅行保険(りょこうほけん)

traveler; tourist **ryokō-sha** 旅行者(りょこうしゃ)

trunk (of a car) **toranku** トランク

try **itte mite** 行(い)ってみて

Tuesday **Ka-yōbi** 火曜日(かようび)

tuna **maguro** まぐろ

twin room **tsuin** ツイン

typhoon **taifū** 台風(たいふう)

U

Ueno Park **Ueno Kōen** 上野公園(うえのこうえん)

umbrella **kasa** 傘(かさ)

uncle (one's own uncle) **oji** おじ

uncle (someone else's uncle) **oji-san** おじさん

undershirt **shatsu** シャツ

undershort **pantsu** パンツ

underwear **shitagi** 下着(したぎ)

university **daigaku** 大学(だいがく)

up **ue** 上(うえ)

V

vegetable **yasai** 野菜(やさい)

vest **besuto** ベスト

Vietnam **Betonamu** ベトナム

Vietnamese (language; person) **Betonamu-go; Betonamu-jin** ベトナム語(ご); ベトナム人(じん)

view **nagame** 眺(なが)め

vintage **furui** 古(ふる)い

W

waiting room **machiai-shitsu** 待合室(まちあいしつ)

Wakayama (prefecture) **Wakayama-ken** 和歌山県(わかやまけん)

wake me (up) **okoshite kudasai** 起(お)こしてください

walk **arukimahss** 歩(ある)きます

walked **arukimashita** 歩(ある)きました

wallet **saifu** 財布(さいふ)

want **hoshii** ほしい

want to buy **kai-tai** 買(か)いたい

want to do **shi-tai** したい

want to go **iki-tai** 行(い)きたい

want to see **mi-tai** 見(み)たい

want; need **irimahss** いります

warm **atatakai** 暖(あたた)かい

was **deshita** でした

watch (n.) **tokei** 時計(とけい)

watch (v.) **miru; mimahss** 見(み)る; 見(み)ます

water **mizu** 水(みず)

watermelon **suika** すいか

way **michi** 道(みち)

weather **tenki** 天気(てんき)

weather bureau **kishō-dai** 気象台(きしょうだい)

weather forecast **tenki-yohō** 天気予報(てんきよほう)

wedding ceremony **kekkon-shiki** 結婚式(けっこんしき)

Wednesday **Sui-yōbi** 水曜日(すいようび)

week before last **sen-senshū** 先々週(せんせんしゅう)

weekday heijitsu 平日(へ
いじつ)

weekend shūmatsu 週末
(しゅうまつ)

welcome party kangei-kai
歓迎会(かんげいかい)

well yoku よく

well then dewa では

went ikimashita 行(い)き
ました

were deshita でした

west nishi 西 (にし)

what nan; nani 何(なん;
なに)

**what day (of the month)
nan-nichi** 何日(なんにち)

**what day (of the week) nan-
yōbi** 何曜日(なんようび)

**What happened? Dō shima-
shita ka?** どうしましたか?

what kind of don-na どんな

what time nan-ji ni 何時
(なんじ)に

what year nan-nen 何年
(なんねん)

**What's your name? O-
namae wa?** お名前(なま
え)は?

**What's your occupation?
O-shigoto wa?** お仕事(し
ごと)は?

when itsu いつ

when we get there tsuitara
着(つ)いたら

**where doko; doko e; dochi-
ra** どこ; どこへ; どちら

where to doko e どこへ

which dono どの

which one dore どれ

whisky uisukii ウイスキー

**whisky and water uisukii
no mizu-wari** ウイスキー
の水割(みずわ)り

who dare; dochira-sama
誰(だれ); どちら様(さま)

wicket kaisatsu-guchi 改
札口(かいさつぐち)

wife (one's wife) kanai
家内

**wife (someone else's wife)
oku-san** 奥(おく)さん

**will be; will probably be
deshō** でしょう

wind kaze 風(かぜ)

wind chime fūrin 風鈴(ふ
うりん)

wine wain ワイン

winter fuyu 冬(ふゆ)

**winter vacation fuyu-ya-
sumi** 冬休(ふゆやす)み

with what nani de 何(な
に)で

woman onna no hito 女(お
んな)の人(ひと)

woodblock print hanga 版
画(はんが)

write kaku 書(か)く

**wrong number bangō-
chigai** 番号(ばんごう)違
(ちが)い

Y

**Yamagata (prefecture)
Yamagata-ken** 山形県(や
まがたけん)

**Yamaguchi (prefecture)
Yamaguchi-ken** 山口県
(やまぐちけん)

**Yamanashi (prefecture)
Yamanashi-ken** 山梨県
(やまなしけん)

year after next sarainen
再来年(さらいねん)

year before last ototoshi
一昨年(おととし)

yellowtail hamachi はまち

yes hai はい

yesterday kinō 昨日(きのう)

yogurt yōguruto ヨーグルト

you anata あなた

You can use riyō dekimahss
利用(りよう)できます

**You're welcome. Dō-
itashimashite.** どういたし
まして。

younger brother (one's own younger brother) **otōto** 弟(おとうと)

younger brother (someone else's younger brother or brother-in-law) **otōto-san** 弟(おとうと)さん

younger sister (one's own younger sister or sister-in-law) **imōto** 妹(いもうと)

younger sister (someone else's younger sister or sister-in-law) **imōto-san** 妹(いもうと)さん

your **anata no** あなたの

Z

zoo **dōbutsu-en** 動物園(どうぶつえん)

Numerals

1 **ichi** 一(いち)
2 **ni** 二(に)
3 **san** 三(さん)
4 **shi; yon** 四(し; よん)
5 **go** 五(ご)
6 **roku** 六(ろく)
7 **shichi; nana** 七(しち; なな)
8 **hachi** 八(はち)
9 **ku; kyū** 九(く; きゅう)
10 **jū; tō** 十(じゅう; とお)

11 **jū-ichi** 十一(じゅういち)
12 **jū-ni** 十二(じゅうに)
13 **jū-san** 十三(じゅうさん)
14 **jū-shi; jū-yon** 十四(じゅうし; じゅうよん)
15 **jū-go** 十五(じゅうご)
16 **jū-roku** 十六(じゅうろく)
17 **jū-shichi; jū-nana** 十七(じゅうしち; じゅうなな)
18 **jū-hachi** 十八(じゅうはち)
19 **jū-ku; jū-kyū** 十九(じゅうく; じゅうきゅう)
20 **ni-jū** 二十(にじゅう)
21 **ni-jū-ichi** 二十一(にじゅういち)
30 **san-jū** 三十(さんじゅう)
31 **san-jū-ichi** 三十一(さんじゅういち)
40 **yon-jū** 四十(よんじゅう)
50 **go-jū** 五十(ごじゅう)
60 **roku-jū** 六十(ろくじゅう)
70 **shichi-jū; nana-jū** 七十(しちじゅう; ななじゅう)
80 **hachi-jū** 八十(はちじゅう)
90 **kyū-jū** 九十(きゅうじゅう)
100 **hyaku** 百(ひゃく)
101 **hyaku-ichi** 百一(ひゃくいち)

110 **hyaku-jū** 百十(ひゃくじゅう)
200 **ni-hyaku** 二百(にひゃく)
300 **san-byaku** 三百(さんびゃく)
400 **yon-hyaku** 四百(よんひゃく)
500 **go-hyaku** 五百(ごひゃく)
600 **rop-pyaku** 六百(ろっぴゃく)
700 **nana-hyaku** 七百(ななひゃく)
800 **hap-pyaku** 八百(はっぴゃく)
900 **kyū-hyaku** 九百(きゅうひゃく)
1,000 **sen** 千(せん)
2,000 **ni-sen** 二千(にせん)
3,000 **san-zen** 三千(さんぜん)
4,000 **yon-sen** 四千(よんせん)
5,000 **go-sen** 五千(ごせん)
6,000 **roku-sen** 六千(ろくせん)
7,000 **nana-sen** 七千(ななせん)
8,000 **has-sen** 八千(はっせん)

9,000 **kyū-sen** 九千(きゅうせん)

10,000 **ichi-man** 一万(いちまん)

100,000 **jū-man** 十万(じゅうまん)

1,000,000 **hyaku-man** 百万(ひゃくまん)

How to count things

one (of these) **hitotsu** 1つ(ひとつ)

two **futatsu** 2つ(ふたつ)

three **mittsu** 3つ(みっつ)

four **yottsu** 4つ(よっつ)

five **itsutsu** 5つ(いつつ)

six **muttsu** 6つ(むっつ)

seven **nanatsu** 7つ(ななつ)

eight **yattsu** 8つ(やっつ)

nine **kokonotsu** 9つ(ここのつ)

ten pieces **jukko** 10個(じゅっこ)

How to count people

one person **hitori** 1人; 一人(ひとり)

two people **futari** 2人; 二人(ふたり)

three people **san-nin** 3人; 三人(さんにん)

four people **yo-nin** 4人; 四人(よにん)

five people **go-nin** 5人; 五人(ごにん)

six people **roku-nin** 6人; 六人(ろくにん)

seven people **shichi-nin; nana-nin** 7人; 七人(しちにん; ななにん)

eight people **hachi-nin** 8人; 八人(はちにん)

nine people **kyū-nin; ku-nin** 9人; 九人(きゅうにん; くにん)

ten people **jū-nin** 10人; 十人(じゅうにん)

Years

1990 **sen-kyū-hyaku kyū-jū-nen** 1990年(せんきゅうひゃくきゅうじゅうねん)

2000 **nisen-nen** 2000年(にせんねん)

2001 **nisen-ichi-nen** 2001年(にせんいちねん)

2017 **nisen-jū-nana-nen; nisen-jū-shichi-nen** 2017年(にせんじゅうななねん; にせんじゅうしちねん)

Months

January **Ichi-gatsu** 1月(いちがつ)

February **Ni-gatsu** 2月(にがつ)

March **San-gatsu** 3月(さんがつ)

April **Shi-gatsu** 4月(しがつ)

May **Go-gatsu** 5月(ごがつ)

June **Roku-gatsu** 6月(ろくがつ)

July **Shichi-gatsu** 7月(しちがつ)

August **Hachi-gatsu** 8月(はちがつ)

September **Ku-gatsu** 9月(くがつ)

October **Jū-gatsu** 10月(じゅうがつ)

November **Jū-ichi-gatsu** 11月(じゅういちがつ)

December **Jū-ni-gatsu** 12月(じゅうにがつ)

Days

the 1st **tsuitachi** 1日(ついたち)

the 2nd **futsuka** 2日(ふつか)

the 3rd **mikka** 3日(みっか)

the 4th **yokka** 4日(よっか)

the 5th **itsuka** 5日(いつか)

the 6th **muika** 6日(むいか)
the 7th **nanoka** 7日(なのか)
the 8th **yōka** 8日(よおか)
the 9th **kokonoka** 9日(こ
このか)
the 10th **tōka** 10日(とおか)
the 11th **jū-ichi-nichi** 11日
(じゅういちにち)
the 12th **jū-ni-nichi** 12日
(じゅうににち)
the 13th **jū-san-nichi** 13日
(じゅうさんにち)
the 14th **jū-yokka** 14日(じ
ゅうよっか)
the 15th **jū-go-nichi** 15日
(じゅうごにち)
the 16th **jū-roku-nichi** 16
日(じゅうろくにち)
the 17th **jū-shichi-nichi** 17
日(じゅうしちにち)
the 18th **jū-hachi-nichi** 18
日(じゅうはちにち)
the 19th **jū-ku-nichi** 19日
(じゅうくにち)
the 20th **hatsuka** 20日(は
つか)
the 21st **ni-jū-ichi-nichi**
21日(にじゅういちにち)
the 22nd **ni-jū-ni-nichi**
22日(にじゅうににち)
the 23rd **ni-jū-san-nichi**
23日(にじゅうさんにち)

the 24th **ni-jū-yokka** 24日
(にじゅうよっか)
the 25th **ni-jū-go-nichi** 25
日(にじゅうごにち)
the 26th **ni-jū-roku-nichi**
26日(にじゅうろくにち)
the 27th **ni-jū-shichi-nichi**
27日(にじゅうしちにち)
the 28th **ni-jū-hachi-nichi**
28日(にじゅうはちにち)
the 29th **ni-jū-ku-nichi**
29日(にじゅうくにち)
the 30th **san-jū-nichi** 30日
(さんじゅうにち)
the 31st **san-jū-ichi-nichi**
31日(さんじゅういちにち)

Minutes

one minute **ip-pun** 1分(い
っぷん)
two minutes **ni-fun** 2分
(にふん)
three minutes **san-pun**
3分(さんぷん)
four minutes **yon-pun** 4分
(よんぷん)
five minutes **go-fun** 5分
(ごふん)
six minutes **rop-pun** 6分
(ろっぷん)
seven minutes **nana-fun**
7分(ななふん)

eight minutes **hachi-fun**;
hap-pun 8分(はちふん;
はっぷん)
nine minutes **kyū-fun** 9分
(きゅうふん)
ten minutes **jip-pun**; **jup-
pun** 10分 (じっぷん; じゅ
っぷん)

Number of nights

overnight stay **ip-paku**
1泊(いっぱく)
two-night stay **ni-haku**
2泊(にはく)
three-night stay **san-paku**
3泊(さんぱく)
four-night stay **yon-haku**
4泊(よんはく)
five-night stay **go-haku**
5泊(ごはく)
six-night stay **rop-paku**
6泊(ろっぱく)
seven-night stay **nana-
haku** 7泊(ななはく)
eight-night stay **hap-paku**
8泊(はっぱく)
nine-night stay **kyū-haku**
9泊(きゅうはく)
ten-night stay **jup-paku**;
jip-paku 10泊(じゅっぱ
く; じっぱく)

Japanese-English Dictionary

A

愛知県(あいちけん) **Aichi-ken** Aichi (prefecture)

アイディーカード **aidii kado** ID card

アイスクリーム **aisu-kurii-mu** ice cream

味(あじ) **aji** taste

赤信号(あかしんごう) **aka-shingō** red light

赤帽(あかぼう) **akabō** porter

秋(あき) **aki** autumn

秋田県(あきたけん) **Aki-ta-ken** Akita (prefecture)

甘(あま)い **amai** sweet

雨(あめ) **ame** rain; rainy

アメリカ **Amerika** The United States

アメリカ人(じん) **Amerika-jin** American (person)

あなた **anata** you

あなたの **anata no** your

姉(あね) **ane** older sister (one's own older sister or sister-in-law)

兄(あに) **ani** older brother (one's own older brother or brother-in-law)

案内所(あんないじょ) **annai-jo** information office

あの **ano** that

あの人(ひと) **ano hito** that person

あの角(かど)で **ano kado de** at that corner

青信号(あおしんごう) **ao-shingō** green light

青森県(あおもりけん) **Aomori-ken** Aomori (prefecture)

嵐(あらし) **arashi** storm

あれ **are** that; that one

あります **arimahss** there is; there are

ありません **arimasen** don't have

歩(ある)きました **aruki-mashita** walked

歩(ある)きます **arukimahss** walk

朝(あさ)ごはん **asa-gohan** breakfast

明後日(あさって) **asatte** the day after tomorrow

足(あし); 脚(あし) **ashi** foot; leg

明日(あした) **ashita** tomorrow

明日(あした)の朝(あさ) **ashita no asa** tomorrow morning

あそこ **asoko** over there; that place

頭(あたま) **atama** head

新(あたら)しい **atarashii** new; fresh

暖(あたた)かい **atatakai** warm

熱(あつ)い **atsui** hot

暑(あつ)い日(ひ) **atsui hi** hot day

鮮(あざ)やかな **azayaka-na** bright

B

…番 **… ban** (number) …

…番ホーム **… ban hōmu** platform (number) …

…番のバス **… ban no basu** bus (number) …

…番線(ばんせん) **… ban-sen** track (number) …

晩(ばん)ごはん **ban-gohan** supper

番号(ばんごう)違(ちが)い **bangō-chigai** wrong number

バス **basu** bus

バスルーム **basu-rūmu** bathroom

バス停(てい) **basu-tei** bus stop

バス付(つ)きの部屋(へや) **basu-tsuki no heya** room with a bathroom

弁護士(べんごし) **bengo-shi** lawyer

ベスト **besuto** vest

ベトナム **Betonamu** Vietnam

ベトナム語(ご) **Betonamu-go** Vietnamese (language)

ベトナム人(じん) **Beto-namu-jin** Vietnamese (people)

ビール **biiru** beer

美術館(びじゅつかん) **bijutsu-kan** art museum

ビル **biru** building

盆栽(ぼんさい) **bonsai** Bonsai (miniature potted tree or shrub)

帽子(ぼうし) **bōshi** cap; hat

ぶどう **budō** grape

豚肉(ぶたにく) **buta-niku** pork

仏像(ぶつぞう) **butsuzō** statue of a Buddha

ブザー **buzā** buzzer (to get off)

病院(びょういん) **byōin** hospital

C

茶畑(ちゃばたけ) **cha-batake** tea field

茶碗(ちゃわん) **chawan** rice bowl

千葉県(ちばけん) **Chiba-ken** Chiba (prefecture)

父(ちち) **chichi** father (one's own father)

違(ちが)います。 **Chigai-mahss.** No, I'm not.

小(ちい)さい **chiisai** small

地下(ちか) **chika** basement

地下鉄(ちかてつ) **chika-tetsu** subway

地下鉄(ちかてつ)の駅(えき) **chika-tetsu no eki** subway station

近(ちか)い **chikai** near

近(ちか)いうちに **chikai uchi ni** one of these days

地図(ちず) **chizu** map

地図(ちず)で **chizu de** on the map

提灯(ちょうちん) **chōchin** lantern

彫刻(ちょうこく) **chōkoku** sculpture

長距離電話(ちょうきょりでんわ) **chōkyori-denwa** long distance telephone call

調子(ちょうし)がよくない **chōshi ga yokunai** does not work very well

ちょっと **chotto** a little; a moment

中国(ちゅうごく) **Chūgoku** China

中国語(ちゅうごくご) **Chūgoku-go** Chinese (language)

中国人(ちゅうごくじん) **Chūgoku-jin** Chinese (people)

中国料理(ちゅうごくりょうり); 中華料理(ちゅうかりょうり) **Chūgoku-ryōri; Chūka-ryōri** Chinese cuisine

中央(ちゅうおう)に **chūō ni** in the middle of

中央線(ちゅうおうせん) **Chūō-sen** Chuo Line (train line from Tokyo to Nagano Prefecture)

注射(ちゅうしゃ) **chūsha** injection; shot

駐車場(ちゅうしゃじょう) **chūsha-jō** parking lot

D

ダブルルーム **daburu-rūmu** double room

大仏(だいぶつ) **daibutsu** large statue of Buddha

大学(だいがく) **daigaku** college; university

大丈夫(だいじょうぶ) **daijōbu** all right

暖房(だんぼう) **danbō** heater

だんなさん **danna-san** husband (someone else's husband)

団体旅行(だんたいりょこう) **dantai-ryokō** group tour

誰(だれ) **dare** who

でした **deshita** was; were

出口(でぐち) **deguchi** exit

では **dewa** well then

出(で)かけます **dekake-mahss** go out; leave

電化製品(でんかせいひん) **denka-seihin** electrical goods

電車(でんしゃ) **densha** train

電車(でんしゃ)に **densha ni** on the train

伝統的(でんとうてき)な **dentō-teki-na** traditional

電話(でんわ) **denwa** telephone

電話番号(でんわばんごう) **denwa-bangō** telephone number

電話帳(でんわちょう) **denwa-chō** telephone directory

電話料金(でんわりょうきん) **denwa-ryōkin** telephone bill

デパート **depāto** department store

でした **deshita** was; were

でしょう **deshō** will be; will probably be

です **dess** am; are; is

ではありません **dewa arima-sen** am not; aren't; isn't

ではまた。 **Dewa mata.** See you later.

度(ど) **do** degree

どう **dō** how; how about

どうしましたか？ **Dō shimashita ka?** What happened?

どういたしまして。 **Dō-itashimashite.** You're welcome.

どうやって **dō-yatte** how

土曜日(どようび) **Do-yōbi** Saturday

土曜日(どようび)に **Do-yōbi ni** on Saturday

動物園(どうぶつえん) **dōbutsu-en** zoo

どちら **dochira** where

どちら様(さま) **dochira-sama** who (polite)

ドイツ **Doitsu** Germany

ドイツ語(ご) **Doitsu-go** German (language)

ドイツ人(じん) **Doitsu-jin** German (people)

どこ **doko** where

どこへ **doko e** where; where to

どうもありがとう。; ありがとう。 **Dōmo arigatō.; Arigatō.** Thank you.

どんな **don-na** what kind of

どの **dono** which

どれ **dore** which one

道路(どうろ) **dōro** road

泥棒(どろぼう) **dorobō** thief

どうぞ **dōzo** please (do something)

どうぞよろしく。 **Dōzo yoroshiku.** Glad to meet you.

E

へ **e** to

絵(え) **e** painting

絵葉書(えはがき) **e-hagaki** postcard

エアコン **eakon** air conditioner

エビ **ebi** shrimp

愛媛県(えひめけん) **Ehime-ken** Ehime (prefecture)

英語(えいご) **Ei-go** English language

英語(えいご)で **Ei-go de** in English

英語(えいご)で話(はな)してください。 **Ei-go de hanashite kudasai.** Please speak in English.

英語(えいご)を話(はな)す医者(いしゃ) **Ei-go wo hanasu isha** English-speaking doctor

映画(えいが) **eiga** movie

映画館(えいがかん) **eiga-kan** movie theater

駅(えき) **eki** station; train station

駅(えき)の売店(ばいてん) **eki no baiten** station shop

駅弁(えきべん) **eki-ben** box lunch sold at stations or on trains

駅員(えきいん) **eki-in** station employee

XL(エックスエル); LL(エルエル) **ekkusu-eru** extra large (for clothes)

M(エム) **emu** medium (for clothes)

宴会(えんかい) **enkai** banquet

エレベーター **erebētā** elevator

L(える) **eru** large (for clothes)

S(えす) **esu** small (for clothes)

エスカレーター **esukarētā** escalator

F

ファストフード店(てん) **fasuto fūdo ten** fast food restaurant

フェリー **ferii** ferry

フォーク **fōku** fork

富士山(ふじさん)へ **Fuji-san e** to Mount Fuji

富士山(ふじさん) **Fujisan** Mount Fuji

福井県(ふくいけん) **Fukui-ken** Fukui (prefecture)

福岡県(ふくおかけん) **Fukuoka-ken** Fukuoka (prefecture)

福島県(ふくしまけん) **Fukushima-ken** Fukushima (prefecture)

船(ふね) **fune** ship

フランス **Furansu** France

フランス語(ご) **Furansu-go** French (language)

フランス人(じん) **Furansu-jin** French (people)

降(ふ)ります **furimahss** fall (rain, snow)

風鈴(ふうりん) **fūrin** wind chime

フロント **furonto** front desk; reception desk

風呂敷(ふろしき) **furoshiki** cloth used for wrapping things

古(ふる)い **furui** old; stale; vintage

フルーツ **furūtsu** fruit

普通(ふつう) **futsū** local train

冬(ふゆ) **fuyu** winter

冬休(ふゆやす)み **fuyu-yasumi** winter vacation

G

が **ga** [subject particle]

ガイドブック **gaido-bukku** guidebook

学生(がくせい) **gakusei** student

画廊(がろう) **garō** gallery

ガソリンスタンド **gasorin-sutando** gas station

劇場(げきじょう) **gekijō** theater

元気(げんき) **genki** fine; healthy

下痢(げり) **geri** diarrhea

月曜日(げつようび) **Getsu-yōbi** Monday

岐阜県(ぎふけん) **Gifu-ken** Gifu (prefecture)

ギフトショップ **gifuto-shoppu** gift shop

銀閣寺(ぎんかくじ) **Ginkaku-ji** The Silver Pavilion

銀行(ぎんこう) **ginkō** bank

銀座(ぎんざ) **Ginza** Ginza

銀座(ぎんざ)まで **Ginza made** to Ginza

碁(ご) **go** go (board game played with black and white stones)

号車(ごうしゃ) **gō-sha** car (number)

ごちそうさまでした。 **Gochisō-sama deshita.** Thank you. (It was delicious.)

午後(ごご) **gogo** p.m.

ごはん **gohan** cooked rice; meal

ゴルフのコンペ **gorufu no konpe** golf tournament

午前(ごぜん) **gozen** a.m.

具合(ぐあい)が悪(わる)い **guai ga warui** sick

群馬県(ぐんまけん) **Gunma-ken** Gunma (prefecture)

牛肉(ぎゅうにく) **gyū-niku** beef

牛乳(ぎゅうにゅう) **gyū-nyū** milk

H

歯(は) **ha** tooth

派手(はで)な **hade-na** flashy; gaudy

母(はは) **haha** mother (one's own mother or mother-in-law)

はい **hai** yes

ハイキング **haikingu** hiking

端(はじ)に **haji ni** at the end of

始(はじ)まります **hajima-rimahss** start

はじめまして。 **Hajime-mashite.** How do you do?

博物館(はくぶつかん) **hakubutsu-kan** museum

博覧会(はくらんかい) **hakuran-kai** exposition

はまち **hamachi** yellowtail

半(はん) **han** half (past)

花火(はなび) **hanabi** fireworks

花火大会(はなびたいかい) **hanabi-taikai** fireworks display

花見(はなみ); お花見(はなみ) **hanami; o-hanami** cherry blossom viewing

話(はな)してください **hanashite kudasai** please speak

話(はな)す人(ひと) **hanasu hito** person who speaks

版画(はんが) **hanga** woodblock print

晴(は)れ **hare** fine weather

腫(は)れています **harete imahss** swollen

春(はる) **haru** spring
早(はや)く **hayaku** early
平日(へいじつ) **heijitsu** weekday
閉店時間(へいてんじかん) **heiten-jikan** closing hour of a store
平野(へいや) **heiya** open field; plain
...へたです ...**heta dess** I'm poor at...
部屋(へや) **heya** room
左(ひだり) **hidari** left
左(ひだり)へ **hidari e** to the left
東(ひがし) **higashi** east
ヒーター **hiitā** heater
姫路城(ひめじじょう) **Himeji-jō** Himeji Castle
ひらめ **hirame** flatfish
広場(ひろば) **hiro-ba** public square
広島(ひろしま) **Hiroshima** Hiroshima
広島県(ひろしまけん) **Hiroshima-ken** Hiroshima (prefecture)
昼(ひる)ごはん **hiru-go-han** lunch
秘書(ひしょ) **hisho** secretary
人(ひと) **hito** person

他(ほか)の **hoka-no** different one
北海道(ほっかいどう) **Hokkaidō** Hokkaido (prefecture)
ホーム **hōmu** platform
本(ほん) **hon** book
本屋(ほんや) **hon-ya** bookstore
ほしい **hoshii** want
ホテル **hoteru** hotel
ホテルへ **hoteru e** to the hotel
兵庫県(ひょうごけん) **Hyōgo-ken** Hyogo (prefecture)

I

茨城県(いばらきけん) **Ibaraki-ken** Ibaraki (prefecture)
イギリス **Igirisu** Great Britain, the United Kingdom
イギリス人(じん) **Igirisu-jin** British person
いい **ii** good; nice
いいえ **iie** no
いいえ、けっこうです。 **Iie, kekkō dess.** No, thank you.
いいえ、わかりません。 **Iie, wakarimasen.** No, I don't understand.

イカ **ika** cuttlefish; squid
いかが **ikaga** how about
行(い)けばいいですか? **Ikeba ii dess ka?** Should I go?
行(い)き **-iki** bound for ~
行(い)きたい **iki-tai** want to go
行(い)きます **ikimahss** go
行(い)きません **ikimasen** doesn't go; don't go
イクラ **ikura** salmon roe
いくら **ikura** how much
いくらですか? **Ikura dess ka?** How much is it?
いくつ **ikutsu** how many
今(いま) **ima** now
いません **imasen** aren't in; isn't in
妹(いもうと) **imōto** younger sister (one's own younger sister or sister-in-law)
妹(いもうと)さん **imōto-san** younger sister (someone else's younger sister or sister-in-law)
田舎(いなか) **inaka** country; rural area
稲妻(いなずま) **inazuma** lightning

インドネシア語(ご) **In-doneshia-go** Indonesian (language)

インドネシア人(じん) **In-doneshia-jin** Indonesian (person)

インターネット **Intānetto** the Internet

インターネットカフェ **Inta-netto kafe** Internet café; cyber café

一杯(いっぱい) **ippai** full

入口(いりぐち) **iriguchi** entrance

いります **irimahss** want; need

伊勢神宮(いせじんぐう) **Ise Jingū** Ise Shrine

医者(いしゃ) **isha** doctor

石川県(いしかわけん) **Ishikawa-ken** Ishikawa (prefecture)

痛(いた)い **itai** hurt

イタリア **Itaria** Italy

イタリア語(ご) **Itaria-go** Italian (language)

イタリア人(じん) **Itaria-jin** Italian (person)

いつ **itsu** when

行(い)きました **ikimashita** went

言(い)ってください **itte kudasai** please say

行(い)ってください **itte kudasai** please go

行(い)ってみて **itte mite** try

いわし **iwashi** horse mackerel; sardine

岩手県(いわてけん) **Iwate-ken** Iwate (prefecture)

出雲大社(いずもたいしゃ) **Izumo Taisha** Izumo Shrine

J

じゃがいも **jagaimo** potato

ジェイアールパス **Jei Āru Pass** JR Pass

…時間(じかん) **…jikan** hour(s)

時刻表(じこくひょう) **jikoku-hyō** timetable

地味(じみ)な **jimi-na** refined; subdued

神社(じんじゃ) **jinja** Shinto shrine

地震(じしん) **jishin** earthquake

自由席(じゆうせき) **jiyū-seki** non-reserved seat

K

か **ka** [question particle]

火曜日(かようび) **Ka-yōbi** Tuesday

かぼちゃ **kabocha** pumpkin

歌舞伎(かぶき) **Kabuki** Kabuki

歌舞伎座(かぶきざ) **Kabuki-za** the Kabuki Theater

カーデガン **kādegan** cardigan

角(かど) **kado** corner

帰(かえ)る **kaeru** return

帰(かえ)ります **kaerimahss** return

香川県(かがわけん) **Kagawa-ken** Kagawa (prefecture)

鍵(かぎ) **kagi** key

鹿児島県(かごしまけん) **Kagoshima-ken** Kagoshima (prefecture)

階(かい) **kai** floor

買(か)いたい **kai-tai** want to buy

階段(かいだん) **kaidan** stairs

開演時間(かいえんじかん) **kaien-jikan** the time a performance starts

海外旅行(かいがいりょこう) **kaigai-ryokō** overseas travel

買(か)います **kaimahss** buy

解散時間(かいさんじかん) **kaisan-jikan** break-up time; the time a group disperses

改札口(かいさつぐち) **kaisatsu-guchi** ticket gate; wicket

会社員(かいしゃいん) **kaisha-in** company employee

快速(かいそく) **kaisoku** rapid train

書(か)いてください **kaite kudasai** please write

開店時間(かいてんじかん) **kaiten-jikan** opening hour of a store

掛(か)け物(もの) **kake-mono** hanging picture; hanging scroll

柿(かき) **kaki** persimmon

書(か)きます **kakimahss** write

牡蠣養殖場(かきようしょくじょう) **kaki-yōshokujō** oyster bed (cultivated)

書(か)く **kaku** write

カクテルパーティー **kakuteru-pātii** cocktail party

カメラ **kamera** camera

カメラ屋(や) **kamera-ya** camera shop

雷(かみなり) **kaminari** thunder

カナダ **Kanada** Canada

カナダ人(じん) **Kanada-jin** Canadian

神奈川県(かながわけん) **Kanagawa-ken** Kanagawa (prefecture)

家内 **kanai** wife (one's wife)

神田(かんだ) **Kanda** Kanda (place name in Tokyo)

歓迎会(かんげいかい) **kangei-kai** welcome party

看護婦(かんごふ) **kango-fu** nurse

観光(かんこう) **kankō** sightseeing

観光(かんこう)バス **kankō-basu** tour bus

韓国(かんこく) **Kankoku** Korea (ROK)

韓国語(かんこくご) **Kankoku-go** Korean (language)

韓国人(かんこくじん) **Kankoku-jin** Korean (person)

彼女(かのじょ) **kanojo** she

漢方薬(かんぽうやく) **kanpō-yaku** Chinese medicine

辛(から)い **karai** spicy

彼(かれ) **kare** he

カレーライス **karē-raisu** curry with rice

カレンダー **karendā** calendar

軽(かる)い **karui** light

傘(かさ) **kasa** umbrella

華氏(かし) **Kashi** Fahrenheit

華氏(かし)70度(ななじゅうど) **Kashi nana-jū-do** 70 degrees Fahrenheit

固(かた)い **katai** hard; tough

片道(かたみち)(切符(きっぷ)) **katamichi (-kippu)** one-way (ticket)

かつお **katsuo** bonito

買(か)った **katta** bought

川(かわ) **kawa** river

風(かぜ) **kaze** wind

風邪(かぜ) **kaze** cold

風邪薬(かぜぐすり) **kaze-gusuri** cold medicine

けが **kega** injury

警察署(けいさつしょ) **kei-satsu-sho** police station

携帯(けいたい); 携帯電話 (けいたいでんわ) **keitai; keitai denwa** cell phone

ケーキ **kēki** cake

結婚式(けっこんしき) **kekkon-shiki** wedding ceremony

県(けん) **ken** prefecture

見学旅行(けんがくりょこう) **kengaku-ryokō** field trip; factory tour etc.

気候(きこう) **kikō** climate

聞(き)こえません **kikoe-masen** can't hear

聞(き)きます **kikimahss** listen

聞(き)く **kiku** listen

着物(きもの) **kimono** kimono

金曜日(きんようび) **Kin-yōbi** Friday

禁煙車(きんえんしゃ) **kin'en-sha** non-smoking car

記念日(きねんび) **kinen-bi** anniversary

記念碑(きねんひ) **kinen-hi** monument

金閣寺(きんかくじ) **Kinkaku-ji** The Golden Pavilion

昨日(きのう) **kinō** yesterday

絹(きぬ) **kinu** silk

キヨスク **kiosuku** kiosk

切符(きっぷ) **kippu** ticket

切符(きっぷ)の自動販売機 (じどうはんばいき) **kippu no jidō-hanbaiki** ticket machine

きれいな **kirei-na** pretty

霧(きり) **kiri** fog

季節(きせつ) **kisetsu** season

記者(きしゃ) **kisha** journalist; reporter

気象台(きしょうだい) **kishō-dai** weather bureau

喫茶店(きっさてん) **kissaten** coffee shop

北(きた) **kita** north

切手(きって) **kitte** stamp

清水寺(きよみずでら) **Kiyomizu-dera** Kiyomizu-dera Temple

交番(こうばん) **kōban** police box

紅茶(こうちゃ) **kōcha** black tea

高知県(こうちけん) **Kōchi-ken** Kochi (prefecture)

こちらこそ(よろしく)。 **Kochira koso (yoroshiku).** Glad to meet you, too.

子(こ)ども **kodomo** child

公園(こうえん) **kōen** park

公園(こうえん)まで **kōen made** to the park

コーヒー **kōhii** coffee

コカコーラ **Koka-kōra** Coca-Cola

交換手(こうかんしゅ) **kōkan-shu** operator

ここ **koko** here; this place

ここで **koko de** here

ここは **koko wa** here

ここをまっすぐ **koko wo massugu** straight ahead

国際電話(こくさいでんわ) **kokusai-denwa** international telephone call

皇居(こうきょ) **Kōkyo** the Imperial Palace

困(こま)って **komatte** in trouble

今晩(こんばん) **konban** this evening; tonight

こんばんは。 **Konbanwa.** Good evening.

コンビニ **konbini** convenience store

今月(こんげつ) **kongetsu** this month

こんにちは。 **Konnichiwa.** Hello; Good afternoon.

この **kono** this

この電車(でんしゃ) **kono densha** this train

このへんに **kono hen ni** around here; in this vicinity

この時計(とけい) **kono tokei** this watch

コンサート **konsāto** concert

今週(こんしゅう) **konshū** this week

コップ **koppu** cup; glass

これ **kore** this

これを1つ(ひとつ);このうちのひとつ **kore wo hitotsu; kono uchi no hitotsu** one of these

これを洗濯(せんたく)してもらう **kore wo sentaku shitemorau** have this laundered

氷(こおり) **kōri** ice

交差点(こうさてん) **kōsaten** intersection

公衆電話(こうしゅうでんわ) **kōshū-denwa** public telephone

高層(こうそう)ビル **kōsō-biru** skyscraper

高速道路(こうそくどうろ) **kōsoku-dōro** expressway

コート **kōto** coat

今年(ことし) **kotoshi** this year

骨董品(こっとうひん) **kottō-hin** antique

果物(くだもの) **kudamono** fruit

ください **kudasai** please; please give

クッキー **kukkii** cookie

空港(くうこう) **kūkō** airport

熊本県(くまもとけん) **Kumamoto-ken** Kumamoto (prefecture)

曇(くも)り **kumori** cloudy

クーラー **kūrā** air conditioner

クレジットカード **kurejitto kādo** credit card

薬(くすり) **kusuri** medicine

薬屋(くすりや) **kusuri-ya** pharmacy

靴下(くつした) **kutsushita** sock(s)

くずしてください **kuzushi-te kudasai** please break (into change)

キャベツ **kyabetsu** cabbage

キャンプ **kyanpu** camping

キャッシュカード **kyasshu kādo** ATM card

今日(きょう) **kyō** today

教会(きょうかい) **kyōkai** church

去年(きょねん) **kyonen** last year

京都(きょうと) **Kyōto** Kyoto

京都(きょうと)で **Kyōto de** in Kyoto

京都(きょうと)へ **Kyōto e** to Kyoto

京都(きょうと)まで **Kyōto made** as far as Kyoto; to Kyoto

京都府(きょうとふ) **Kyōto-fu** Kyoto (prefecture)

休暇(きゅうか) **kyūka** day off from work

急行(きゅうこう) **kyūkō** express

救急車(きゅうきゅうしゃ) **kyūkyū-sha** ambulance

きゅうり **kyūri** cucumber

九州(きゅうしゅう)めぐり **Kyūshū-meguri** tour of Kyushu

M

町(まち) **machi** city; town

待合室(まちあいしつ) **machiai-shitsu** waiting room

まで **made** as far as; to

前(まえ) **mae** before; in front

前(まえ)の日(ひ) **mae no hi** previous day

曲(ま)がってください **magatte kudasai** please turn

孫(まご) **mago** grandchild (one's own grandchild)

まぐろ **maguro** tuna

毎晩(まいばん) **mai-ban** every night

毎月(まいげつ; まいつき) **mai-getsu; mai-tsuki** every month

毎年(まいねん; まいとし) **mai-nen; mai-toshi** every year

毎日(まいにち) **mai-nichi** every day

毎週(まいしゅう) **mai-shū** every week

麻雀(マアジャン) **mājan** mahjong

マメ **mame** blister

漫画喫茶(まんがきっさ) **manga kissa** manga café; comic café

満席(まんせき) **manseki** full; no vacancy

丸(まる)い **marui** round

また **mata** again

待(ま)ってください **matte kudasai** please wait

迷(まよ)いました **mayo-imashita** lost (the way)

めぐり **meguri** tour of

明治神宮(めいじじんぐう) **Meiji Jingū** Meiji Shrine

名産(めいさん) **meisan** regional specialty

名所(めいしょ) **meisho** place of interest (tourist attractions)

メロン **meron** melon

メッセージ **messēji** message

目覚(めざ)まし時計(どけい) **mezamashi-dokei** alarm clock

見(み)たい **mi-tai** want to see

身分証明書(みぶんしょうめいしょ) **mibun shōmeisho** ID card

道(みち) **michi** road; street; way

三重県(みえけん) **Mie-ken** Mie (prefecture)

右(みぎ) **migi** right

右(みぎ)へ **migi e** to the right

みかん **mikan** tangerine

見(み)ます **mimahss** see

南(みなみ) **minami** south

民芸品(みんげいひん) **min-gei-hin** folk-art handicraft

見(み)る **miru** watch

店(みせ) **mise** store

見(み)せてください **misete kudasai** please show

味噌(みそ) **miso** miso (bean paste)

見(み)ました **mimashita** saw

宮城県(みやぎけん) **Miyagi-ken** Miyagi (prefecture)

宮崎県(みやざきけん) **Miyazaki-ken** Miyazaki (prefecture)

水(みず) **mizu** water

湖(みずうみ) **mizuumi** lake

もう一度(いちど) **mō ichi-do** once more

もう一度(いちど)、言(い)ってください。 **Mō ichido itte kudasai.** Please say it once more.

もうすぐ **mō sugu** shortly; soon

木曜日(もくようび) **Moku-yōbi** Thursday

桃(もも) **momo** peach

もしもし。 **Moshi-moshi.** Hello. (on the telephone)

もっと **motto** more; some more

もっといい **motto ii** better

もっと大(おお)きい **motto ōkii** bigger

無料(むりょう); 無料(むりょう)で **muryō; muryō de** no charge; for free

蒸(む)し暑(あつ)い **mushi-atsui** humid

息子(むすこ) **musuko** son (one's own son or son-in-law)

息子(むすこ)さん **musuko-san** son (someone else's son or son-in-law)

娘(むすめ) **musume** daughter (one's own daughter or daughter-in-law)

娘(むすめ)さん **musume-san** daughter (someone else's daughter or daughter-in-law)

N

眺(なが)め **nagame** view

長野県(ながのけん) **Nagano-ken** Nagano (prefecture)

長崎県(ながさきけん) **Nagasaki-ken** Nagasaki (prefecture)

内線(ないせん) **naisen** extension

中(なか) **naka** in, inside

なくしました **nakushi-mashita** lost

生(なま) **nama** raw

名前(なまえ) **namae** name

何時(なんじ); 何時(なんじ)に **nan-ji; nan-ji ni** what time

何名様(なんめいさま) **nan-mei-sama** how many people

何年(なんねん) **nan-nen** what year

何日(なんにち) **nan-nichi** what day (of the month)

何曜日(なんようび) **nan-yōbi** what day of the week

何曜日(なんようび)に **nan-yōbi ni** on what day of the week

何(なん; なに) **nan; nani** what

何(なに)で **nani de** with what

ナプキン **napukin** napkin

奈良(なら) **Nara** Nara

奈良(なら)で **Nara de** in Nara

奈良(なら)へ **Nara e** to Nara

奈良県(ならけん) **Nara-ken** Nara (prefecture)

梨(なし) **nashi** pear

なす **nasu** eggplant

夏(なつ) **natsu** summer

夏休(なつやす)み **natsu-yasumi** summer vacation

ね? **Ne?** Isn't it?

値段(ねだん) **nedan** price

熱(ねつ) **netsu** fever

に止(と)まります **ni toma-rimahss** stop at

日曜日(にちようび) **Nichi-yōbi** Sunday

苦(にが)い **nigai** bitter

日本人形(にほんにんぎょう) **Nihon ningyō** Japanese doll

日本語(にほんご) **Nihon-go** Japanese (language)

日本語(にほんご)で **Nihon-go de** in Japanese

日本人(にほんじん) **Nihon-jin** Japanese (person)

日本海(にほんかい) **Nihon-kai** the Sea of Japan

日本料理(にほんりょうり) **Nihon-ryōri** Japanese cuisine

新潟県(にいがたけん) **Niigata-ken** Niigata (prefecture)

二条城(にじょうじょう) **Nijō-jō** Nijo Castle

日光東照宮(にっこうとうしょうぐう) **Nikkō Tōshōgū** Toshogu Shrine

肉(にく) **niku** meat

荷物(にもつ) **nimotsu** bag; baggage

荷物(にもつ)がたくさんあります。 **Nimotsu ga takusan arimahss.** I have many bags.

人(にん) **nin** [suffix to count more than two people]

にんじん **ninjin** carrot

西(にし) **nishi** west

庭(にわ) **niwa** garden

にわか雨(あめ) **niwaka-ame** shower

の **no** of

～の後(あと)(で) **no ato (de)** after ~

の前(まえ)(に) **no mae (ni)** before

海苔(のり) **nori** seaweed

乗(の)り場(ば) **nori-ba** entrance to board; landing

乗(の)り換(か)え **nori-kae** transfer

塗(ぬ)り物(もの) **nuri-mono** lacquerware

盗(ぬす)みました **nusumi-mashita** stole

入場券(にゅうじょうけん) **nyūjō-ken** admission ticket

入場料(にゅうじょうりょう) **nyūjō-ryō** admission fee

O

お **o-** [honorific prefix]

お茶(ちゃ) **o-cha** green tea

お茶(ちゃ)の時間(じかん) **o-cha no jikan** teatime

お電話(でんわ) **o-denwa** telephone

お電話(でんわ)します **o-denwa shimahss** make a telephone call

お風呂(ふろ) **o-furo** bath (communal bath)

お元気(げんき)ですか？ **O-genki dess ka?** How are you?

お箸(はし) **o-hashi** chopsticks

お部屋(へや)で **o-heya de** in your room

お金(かね) **o-kane** money

お勘定(かんじょう) **o-kan-jo** bill; check

お菓子(かし) **o-kashi** sweets

お待(ま)ちください **o-machi kudasai** please wait

お孫(まご)さん **o-mago-san** grandchild (someone else's grandchild)

おまんじゅう **o-manjū** bun with bean-jam filling

お祭(まつ)り **o-matsuri** festival

お土産(みやげ) **o-miyage** souvenir

お腹(なか) **o-naka** stomach

お腹(なか)が一杯(いっぱい)です。 **O-naka ga ip-pai dess.** I'm full.

お名前(なまえ)は？ **O-namae wa?** What's your name?

お願(ねが)いします **o-negai shimahss** please

お飲物(のみもの) **o-nomi-mono** drink

お酒(さけ) **o-sake** saké (Japanese rice wine)

おしぼり **o-shibori** hot or cold hand towel used to wipe one's hands before eating

お仕事(しごと)は？ **O-shigoto wa?** What's your occupation?

お城(しろ) **o-shiro** castle

お葬式(そうしき) **o-sōshiki** funeral

お吸(す)い物(もの) **o-sui-mono** soup

お寿司(すし) **o-sushi** sushi (vinegared rice and raw fish)

お手洗(てあらい) **o-tearai** restroom

お寺(てら) **o-tera** Buddhist temple

おば **oba** aunt (one's own aunt)

おばさん **oba-san** aunt (someone else's aunt)

往復(おうふく)(切符(きっぷ)) **ōfuku (-kippu)** round-trip (ticket)

おはようございます。 **Ohayō gozaimahss.** Good morning.

おいしい **oishii** delicious

おいしいです。 **Oishii dess.** It's delicious.

おいしかったです。 **Oishikatta dess.** It was delicious.

おいしくない **oishiku nai** not tasty

大分県(おおいたけん) **Ōita-ken** Oita (prefecture)

おじ **oji** uncle (one's own uncle)

おじさん **oji-san** uncle (someone else's uncle)

お母(かあ)さん **okā-san** mother (someone else's mother or mother-in-law)

岡山県(おかやまけん) **Okayama-ken** Okayama (prefecture)

大(おお)きい **ōkii** big

大(おお)きいの **ōkii-no** big one

沖縄県(おきなわけん) **Okinawa-ken** Okinawa (prefecture)

起(お)こしてください **okoshite kudasai** wake me (up)

奥(おく)さん **oku-san** wife (someone else's wife)

屋上(おくじょう) **okujō** roof

贈(おく)り物(もの)用(よう)に包(つつ)む **okuri-mono yō ni tsutsumu** gift-wrap

送(おく)ってください **okutte kudasai** please send

おめでとうございます。 **Omedetō gozaimahss.** Congratulations.

お土産(みやげ) **omiyage** souvenir

重(おも)い **omoi** heavy

温度(おんど) **ondo** temperature

お姉(ねえ)さん **onē-san** older sister (someone else's older sister or sister-in-law)

お兄(にい)さん **onii-san** older brother (someone else's older brother or brother-in-law)

女(おんな) **onna** female

女(おんな)の人(ひと) **onna no hito** woman

女(おんな)の子(こ) **onna no ko** girl

温泉(おんせん) **onsen** hot spring

温泉(おんせん)へ **onsen e** to a hot spring

オレンジ **orenji** orange

オレンジジュース **orenji-jūsu** orange juice

織物(おりもの) **ori-mono** cloth; textile

降(お)ろしてください。 **Oroshite kudasai.** Please let me out.

大阪(おおさか) **Ōsaka** Osaka

大阪(おおさか)へ **Ōsaka e** to Osaka

大阪府(おおさかふ) **Ōsaka-fu** Osaka (prefecture)

大阪(おおさか)行(ゆ)き; 行(い)き **Ōsaka-yuki/iki** bound for Osaka

教(おし)えてください **oshi-ete kudasai** please tell

遅(おそ)く **osoku** late

オーストラリア **Ōsutoraria** Australia

オーストラリア人(じん) **Ōsutoraria-jin** Australian

男(おとこ) **otoko** male

男(おとこ)の人(ひと) **oto-ko no hito** man

男(おとこ)の子(こ) **otoko no ko** boy

大人(おとな) **otona** adult

お父(とう)さん **otō-san** father (someone else's father or father-in-law; also used when addressing one's own father)

弟(おとうと) **otōto** younger brother (one's own younger brother)

弟(おとうと)さん **otōto-san** younger brother (someone else's younger brother or brother-in-law)

一昨日(おととい) **ototoi** day before yesterday

一昨年(おととし) **ototoshi** year before last

夫(おっと) **otto** husband (one's husband)

おやすみなさい。**Oyasumi-nasai.** Good night.

P

パン屋(や) **pan-ya** bakery

パンツ **pantsu** pants (trousers); undershort

パソコン **pasokon** personal computer

パスポート **pasupōto** passport

パーティー **pātii** party

ピクニック **pikunikku** picnic

ポケットWi-Fi (ワイファイ) **poketto waifai** pocket Wi-Fi router

ポルトガル **Porutogaru** Portugal

ポルトガル語(ご) **Poru-togaru-go** Portuguese (language)

ポルトガル人(じん) **Poru-togaru-jin** Portuguese (person)

プラットホーム **puratto hōmu** platform

プリペイド携帯(けいたい) **puri peido keitai** prepaid cell phone

R

来月(らいげつ) **raigetsu** next month

来年(らいねん) **rainen** next year

来週(らいしゅう) **raishū** next week

ラジオ **rajio** radio

ラップトップ **rappu toppu** laptop

冷房(れいぼう) **reibō** air conditioner

レインコート **reinkōto** raincoat

レンコン **renkon** lotus root

レストラン **resutoran** restaurant

レタス **retasu** lettuce

りんご **ringo** apple

利用(りよう)できます **riyō dekimahss** You can

ロビー **robii** lobby

廊下(ろうか) **rōka** corridor; hall

ロッカー **rokkā** locker

六本木(ろっぽんぎ) **Rop-pongi** Roppongi

ロシア **Roshia** Russia

ロシア語(ご) **Roshia-go** Russian (language)

ロシア人(じん) **Roshia-jin** Russian (person)

領事館(りょうじかん) **ryōji-kan** consulate

旅館(りょかん) **ryokan** Japanese inn

料金(りょうきん) **ryōkin** charge

旅行保険(りょこうほけん) **ryokō-hoken** travel insurance

旅行(りょこう)センター **ryokō-sentā** travel bureau

旅行者(りょこうしゃ) **ryokō-sha** traveler; tourist

領収書(りょうしゅうしょ) **ryōshū-sho** receipt

S

さば **saba** mackerel

サービス **sābiss** service

サービス料(りょう) **sābisu-ryō** service charge

佐賀県(さがけん) **Saga-ken** Saga (prefecture)

財布(さいふ) **saifu** wallet

祭日(さいじつ) **saijitsu** national holiday

埼玉県(さいたまけん) **Saitama-ken** Saitama (prefecture)

魚(さかな) **sakana** fish

杯(さかずき) **sakazuki** saké cup

さけ **sake** salmon

桜島(さくらじま) **Sakura-jima** Mount Sakurajima

様(さま) **sama** polite equivalent to -san

寒(さむ)い **samui** cold (temperature)

さん **san** (honorific added to another person's name; not used with your own name)

サンドイッチ **sandoitchi** sandwich

山門(さんもん) **sanmon** temple gate

皿(さら) **sara** plate

サラダ **sarada** salad

再来年(さらいねん) **sara-inen** year after next

さようなら。 **Sayōnara.** Goodbye.

線(せん) **sen** line (train)

千円札(せんえんさつ) **sen-en satsu** 1,000-yen note

先々週(せんせんしゅう) **sen-senshū** week before last

せんべい **senbei** rice cracker

先月(せんげつ) **sengetsu** last month

先生(せんせい) **sensei** teacher

先週(せんしゅう) **senshū** last week

浅草寺(せんそうじ) **Sensō-ji** Sensoji Temple

扇子(せんす) **sensu** folding fan

摂氏(せっし) **Sesshi** Celsius

摂氏(せっし)20度(にじゅうど) **Sesshi ni-jū-do** 20 degrees Celsius

セーター **sēta** sweater

瀬戸物(せともの) **seto-mono** pottery

瀬戸内海(せとないかい) **Seto-naikai** Inland Sea

接続(せつぞく) **setsuzoku** connection

写真(しゃしん) **shashin** photo; photograph; picture

車掌(しゃしょう) **shashō** conductor

シャツ **shatsu** shirt; undershirt

したい **shi-tai** want to do

試合(しあい) **shiai** game; match

しばらく **shibaraku** a moment; awhile

滋賀県(しがけん) **Shiga-ken** Shiga (prefecture)

しいたけ **shiitake** shiitake mushroom

鹿(しか) **shika** deer

鹿(しか)の写真(しゃしん) **shika no shashin** photo of deer

四角(しかく)い **shikakui** square

します **shimahss** do

島根県(しまねけん) **Shimane-ken** Shimane (prefecture)

しました **shimashita** did

SIM(シム)カード **shimu kādo** SIM card

市内電話(しないでんわ) **shinai-denwa** local telephone call

市内観光(しないかんこう) **shinai-kankō** tour of a city

新聞(しんぶん) **shinbun** newspaper

新聞(しんぶん)売(う)り場(ば) **shinbun uriba** newspaper stand

信号(しんごう) **shingō** traffic light

シングルルーム **shinguru-rūmu** single room

真珠(しんじゅ) **shinju** pearl

新宿(しんじゅく) **Shinjuku** Shinjuku

新宿(しんじゅく)御苑(ぎょえん) **Shinjuku Gyoen** Shinjuku Gyoen National Garden

新幹線(しんかんせん) **Shinkansen** bullet train

史跡(しせき) **shiseki** historical site

下(した) **shita** down

下着(したぎ) **shitagi** underwear

指定席(していせき) **shitei-seki** reserved seat

静岡県(しずおかけん) **Shizuoka-ken** Shizuoka (prefecture)

焼酎(しょうちゅう) **shōchū** shochu (distilled spirit usually drunk with water or a mixer)

植物園(しょくぶつえん) **shokubutsu-en** botanical garden

食堂(しょくどう) **shokudō** dining hall

食堂車(しょくどうしゃ) **shokudō-sha** dining car

食事(しょくじ) **shokuji** meal

食事(しょくじ)の前(まえ) **shokuji no mae** before a meal

塩(しょ)っぱい **shoppai** salty

集合時間(しゅうごうじかん) **shūgō-jikan** meeting time

週末(しゅうまつ) **shūmatsu** weekend

出発時間(しゅっぱつじかん) **shuppatsu-jikan** departure time

そうです。 **Sō dess.** That's right.

そば **soba** near

そば **soba** buckwheat noodles (dark and thin)

送別会(そうべつかい) **sōbetsu-kai** farewell party

外(そと) **soto** out; outside

スエット **suetto** sweatshirt

すぐ **sugu** right away

水曜日(すいようび) **Sui-yōbi** Wednesday

水田(すいでん) **suiden** rice paddy

すいか **suika** watermelon

空(す)いています **suite-imahss** hungry

スカート **sukāto** skirt

好(す)き **suki** like

好(す)きではありません **suki dewa arimasen** don't like

すき焼(や)き **suki-yaki** popular dish of meat, vegetable, bean curd, etc.

すみませんが… **Sumimasen ga…** Sorry, but…

すみません。**Sumimasen.** Excuse me.

相撲(すもう) **sumō** sumo, traditional Japanese wrestling

スペイン **Supein** Spain

スペイン語(ご) **Supein-go** Spanish (language)

スペイン人(じん) **Supein-jin** Spanish (person)

スポーツ **supōtsu** sports

スポット **supotto** spot

酸(す)っぱい **suppai** sour

スプーン **supūn** spoon

すり **suri** pickpocket

スタジアム **sutajiamu** stadium

涼(すず)しい **suzushii** cool

T

タブレット **taburetto** tablet

たぶん **tabun** probably

たぶん…でしょう **tabun… deshō** It'll probably…

タイ語(ご) **Tai-go** Thai (language)

タイ人(じん) **Tai-jin** Thai (person)

台風(たいふう) **taifū** typhoon

太平洋(たいへいよう) **Taihei-yō** the Pacific Ocean

体温計(たいおんけい) **taion-kei** thermometer

大使館(たいしかん) **taishi-kan** embassy

高(たか)い **takai** expensive

竹(たけ)の子(こ) **takenoko** bamboo shoot

タコ **tako** octopus

たくさん **takusan** many

タクシー **takushii** taxi

タクシー乗(の)り場(ば) **takushii-noriba** taxi stand

玉子(たまご) **tamago** egg

玉(たま)ねぎ **tamanegi** onion

田中(たなか)さん **Tanaka-san** Mr.; Mrs.; Ms.; Miss Tanaka

田中(たなか)さんの **Tanaka-san no** Mr.; Mrs.; Ms.; Miss Tanaka's

誕生日(たんじょうび) **tanjō-bi** birthday

助(たす)けて! **Tasukete!** Help!

手(て) **te** hand

手荷物(てにもつ)一時(いちじ)預り所(あずかりじょ) **te-nimotsu ichiji azukari-jo** baggage checkroom

手袋(てぶくろ) **tebukuro** gloves

手紙(てがみ) **tegami** letter

帝国(ていこく)ホテル **Tei-koku Hoteru** Imperial Hotel

定食(ていしょく) **teishoku** set meal (includes main dish, soup, pickles, and rice)

天気(てんき) **tenki** weather

天気予報(てんきよほう) **tenki-yohō** weather forecast

天(てん)ぷら **tenpura** tempura (deep-fried food)

展覧会(てんらんかい) **tenran-kai** exhibition

テレビ **terebi** television

テレフォンカード **terefon-kādo** telephone card

T(ティー)シャツ **tii-shatsu** T-shirt

塔(とう) **tō** pagoda; tower

到着時間(とうちゃくじかん) **tōchaku-jikan** arrival time

栃木県(とちぎけん) **Tochigi-ken** Tochigi (prefecture)

東大寺(とうだいじ) **Tōdai-ji** Todaiji Temple
豆腐(とうふ) **tōfu** tofu
遠(とお)い **tōi** far
東寺(とうじ) **Tō-ji** Toji Temple
陶磁器(とうじき) **tōjiki** chinaware
時計(とけい) **tokei** clock; watch
徳利(とっくり) **tokkuri** saké bottle
特急(とっきゅう) **Tokkyū** Limited Express
徳島県(とくしまけん) **Tokushima-ken** Tokushima (prefecture)
東京(とうきょう)ディズニーランド **Tōkyō Dizunii rando** Tokyo Disneyland
東京駅(とうきょうえき) **Tōkyō-eki** Tokyo Station
東京(とうきょう)スカイツリー **Tōkyō Sukai Tsurii** Tokyo Sky Tree
東京(とうきょう)タワー **Tōkyō Tawā** Tokyo Tower
東京都(とうきょうと) **Tōkyō-to** Tokyo (prefecture)
トマト **tomato** tomato
止(と)めてください **tomete kudasai** please stop (a car)

友(とも)だち **tomodachi** friend
とうもろこし **tōmorokoshi** corn
とんかつ **tonkatsu** pork cutlet
トランク **toranku** trunk (of a car)
トレーナー **torēnā** sweat-shirt
鳥居(とりい) **torii** Shinto shrine archway
鶏肉(とりにく) **tori-niku** chicken
撮(と)ります **torimahss** take
図書館(としょかん) **tosho-kan** library
撮(と)りました **totta** took
撮(と)ってください **totte kudasai** please take
鳥取県(とっとりけん) **Tottori-ken** Tottori (prefecture)
富山県(とやまけん) **Toyama-ken** Toyama (prefecture)
次(つぎ)の日(ひ) **tsugi no hi** next day
ツイン **tsuin** twin room
着(つ)いたら **tsuitara** when we get there

使(つか)えます **tsukae-mahss** can be used
使(つか)えますか? **Tsu-kaemahss ka?** Can I use...?
漬(つ)け物(もの) **tsuke-mono** pickle
冷(つめ)たい **tsumetai** cold (to the touch)
つながりません **tsunagari-masen** can't connect
つながります **tsunagari-mahss** can connect to...
包(つつ)んでください **tsutsunde kudasai** please wrap

U

うどん **udon** noodles (white and fat)
上(うえ) **ue** up
上野公園(うえのこうえん) **Ueno Kōen** Ueno Park
ウイスキー **uisukii** whisky
ウイスキーの水割(みずわ)り **uisukii no mizu-wari** whisky and water
受付(うけつけ) **uketsuke** reception
海(うみ) **umi** ocean
うな丼(どん) **una-don** broiled eel and rice

運賃表(うんちんひょう) **unchin-hyō** fare table

運動(うんどう) **undō** physical exercise

うに **uni** sea urchin

運転免許証(うんてんめんきょしょう) **unten menkyo-shō** driver's license

後(うし)ろ **ushiro** behind

美(うつく)しい **utsukushii** beautiful

上着(うわぎ) **uwagi** jacket; coat

W

は **wa** [subject particle, to distinguish one noun from another]

ワイン **wain** wine

わかります。**Wakarimahss.** I understand.

わかりません **wakarimasen** don't know; can't find

和歌山県(わかやまけん) **Wakayama-ken** Wakayama (prefecture)

ワンピース **wanpiisu** dress (one-piece suit)

悪(わる)い天気(てんき) **warui tenki** bad weather

和紙(わし) **washi** traditional, handmade paper

私(わたし) **watashi** I

私(わたし)の **watashi no** my

私(わたし)のおごりです。**Watashi no ogori dess.** It's my treat.

を **wo** [direct object particle]

…を買(か)えますか? **wo kaemahss ka?** Can I buy...?

…を借(か)りられますか? **wo kariraremahss ka?** Can I rent...?

Y

焼(や)き鳥(とり) **yaki-tori** grilled, skewered chicken

約束(やくそく) **yakusoku** appointment; engagement; promise

約束(やくそく)の時間(じかん) **yakusoku no jikan** time set for an appointment

薬局(やっきょく) **yakkyoku** pharmacy

野球(やきゅう)の試合(しあい) **yakyū no shiai** baseball game

山(やま) **yama** mountain

山登(やまのぼ)り **yama-nobori** mountain climbing

山形県(やまがたけん) **Yamagata-ken** Yamagata (prefecture)

山口県(やまぐちけん) **Yamaguchi-ken** Yamaguchi (prefecture)

山梨県(やまなしけん) **Yamanashi-ken** Yamanashi (prefecture)

野菜(やさい) **yasai** vegetable

安(やす)い **yasui** cheap; inexpensive

安(やす)いの **yasui-no** inexpensive one

休(やす)み **yasumi** day off; holiday

柔(やわ)らかい **yawarakai** soft; tender

ヨーグルト **yōguruto** yogurt

よく **yoku** well

読(よ)む; 読(よ)みます **yomu; yomimahss** read

呼(よ)んでください **yonde kudasai** please call

予約(よやく) **yoyaku** reservation

湯(ゆ)のみ **yu-nomi** teacup

郵便(ゆうびん) **yūbin** mail

郵便局(ゆうびんきょく) **yūbin-kyoku** post office

遊園地(ゆうえんち) **yūenchi** amusement park

浴衣(ゆかた) **yukata** light cotton kimono

雪(ゆき) **yuki** snow
行(ゆ)き **yuki** bound for ~
ゆっくり **yukkuri** slowly
ゆっくり話(はな)してください。 **Yukkuri hanashite kudasai.** Please speak slowly.
有名(ゆうめい)な **yūmei na** famous
遊覧船(ゆうらんせん) **yūran-sen** excursion boat

Z

座席指定券(ざせきしていけん) **zaseki shitei-ken** reserved-seat ticket
雑誌(ざっし) **zasshi** magazine
税金(ぜいきん) **zeikin** tax
像(ぞう) **zō** statue

Numerals

一(いち) **ichi** 1
二(に) **ni** 2
三(さん) **san** 3
四(し; よん) **shi; yon** 4
五(ご) **go** 5
六(ろく) **roku** 6
七(しち; なな) **shichi; nana** 7
八(はち) **hachi** 8
九(く; きゅう) **ku; kyū** 9
十(じゅう; とお) **jū; tō** 10
十一(じゅういち) **jū-ichi** 11
十二(じゅうに) **jū-ni** 12
十三(じゅうさん) **jū-san** 13
十四(じゅうし; じゅうよん) **jū-shi; jū-yon** 14
十五(じゅうご) **jū-go** 15
十六(じゅうろく) **jū-roku** 16
十七(じゅうしち; じゅうなな) **jū-shichi; jū-nana** 17
十八(じゅうはち) **jū-hachi** 18
十九(じゅうく; じゅうきゅう) **jū-ku; jū-kyū** 19
二十(にじゅう) **ni-jū** 20
二十一(にじゅういち) **ni-jū-ichi** 21
三十(さんじゅう) **san-jū** 30
三十一(さんじゅういち) **san-jū-ichi** 31
四十(よんじゅう) **yon-jū** 40
五十(ごじゅう) **go-jū** 50
六十(ろくじゅう) **roku-jū** 60
七十(しちじゅう; ななじゅう) **shichi-jū; nana-jū** 70
八十(はちじゅう) **hachi-jū** 80
九十(きゅうじゅう) **kyū-jū** 90
百(ひゃく) **hyaku** 100
百一(ひゃくいち) **hyaku-ichi** 101
百十(ひゃくじゅう) **hyaku-jū** 110
二百(にひゃく) **ni-hyaku** 200
三百(さんびゃく) **san-byaku** 300
四百(よんひゃく) **yon-hyaku** 400
五百(ごひゃく) **go-hyaku** 500
六百(ろっぴゃく) **rop-pyaku** 600
七百(ななひゃく) **nana-hyaku** 700
八百(はっぴゃく) **hap-pyaku** 800
九百(きゅうひゃく) **kyū-hyaku** 900
千(せん) **sen** 1,000
二千(にせん) **ni-sen** 2,000
三千(さんぜん) **san-zen** 3,000
四千(よんせん) **yon-sen** 4,000
五千(ごせん) **go-sen** 5,000
六千(ろくせん) **roku-sen** 6,000
七千(ななせん) **nana-sen** 7,000

八千(はっせん) **has-sen** 8,000

九千(きゅうせん) **kyū-sen** 9,000

一万(いちまん) **ichi-man** 10,000

十万(じゅうまん) **jū-man** 100,000

百万(ひゃくまん) **hyaku-man** 1,000,000

How to count things

1つ(ひとつ) **hitotsu** one (of these)

2つ(ふたつ) **futatsu** two

3つ(みっつ) **mittsu** three

4つ(よっつ) **yottsu** four

5つ(いつつ) **itsutsu** five

6つ(むっつ) **muttsu** six

7つ(ななつ) **nanatsu** seven

8つ(やっつ) **yattsu** eight

9つ(ここのつ) **kokonotsu** nine

10個(じゅっこ) **jukko** 10 pieces

How to count people

1人; 一人(ひとり) **hitori** one person

2人; 二人(ふたり) **futari** two people

2人; 三人(さんにん) **san-nin** 3 people

2人; 四人(よにん) **yo-nin** four people

5人; 五人(ごにん) **go-nin** five people

6人; 六人(ろくにん) **roku-nin** six people

7人; 七人(しちにん; ななにん) **shichi-nin; nana-nin** seven people

8人; 八人(はちにん) **ha-chi-nin** eight people

9人; 九人(きゅうにん; くにん) **kyū-nin; ku-nin** nine people

10人; 十人(じゅうにん) **jū-nin** 10 people

Years

1990年(せんきゅうひゃくきゅうじゅうねん) **sen-kyū-hyaku kyū-jū-nen** 1990

2000年(にせんねん) **nisen-nen** 2000

2001年(にせんいちねん) **nisen-ichi-nen** 2001

2017年(にせんじゅうななねん; にせんじゅうしちねん) **nisen-jū-nana-nen; nisen-jū-shichi-nen** 2017

Months

1月(いちがつ) **Ichi-gatsu** January

2月(にがつ) **Ni-gatsu** February

3月(さんがつ) **San-gatsu** March

4月(しがつ) **Shi-gatsu** April

5月(ごがつ) **Go-gatsu** May

6月(ろくがつ) **Roku-gatsu** June

7月(しちがつ) **Shichi-gatsu** July

8月(はちがつ) **Hachi-gatsu** August

9月(くがつ) **Ku-gatsu** September

10月(じゅうがつ) **Jū-gatsu** October

11月(じゅういちがつ) **Jū-ichi-gatsu** November

12月(じゅうにがつ) **Jū-ni-gatsu** December

Days

1日(ついたち) **tsuitachi** the 1st

2日(ふつか) **futsuka** the 2nd

3日(みっか) **mikka** the 3rd

4日(よっか) **yokka** the 4th

5日(いつか) **itsuka** the 5th

6日(むいか) **muika** the 6th
7日(なのか) **nanoka** the 7th
8日(よおか) **yōka** the 8th
9日(ここのか) **kokonoka** the 9th
10日(とおか) **tōka** the 10th
11日(じゅういちにち) **jū-ichi-nichi** the 11th
12日(じゅうににち) **jū-ni-nichi** the 12th
13日(じゅうさんにち) **jū-san-nichi** the 13th
14日(じゅうよっか) **jū-yokka** the 14th
15日(じゅうごにち) **jū-go-nichi** the 15th
16日(じゅうろくにち) **jū-roku-nichi** the 16th
17日(じゅうしちにち) **jū-shichi-nichi** the 17th
18日(じゅうはちにち) **jū-hachi-nichi** the 18th
19日(じゅうくにち) **jū-ku-nichi** the 19th
20日(はつか) **hatsuka** the 20th
21日(にじゅういちにち) **ni-jū-ichi-nichi** the 21st
22日(にじゅうににち) **ni-jū-ni-nichi** the 22nd
23日(にじゅうさんにち) **ni-jū-san-nichi** the 23rd
24日(にじゅうよっか) **ni-jū-yokka** the 24th
25日(にじゅうごにち) **ni-jū-go-nichi** the 25th
26日(にじゅうろくにち) **ni-jū-roku-nichi** the 26th
27日(にじゅうしちにち) **ni-jū-shichi-nichi** the 27th
28日(にじゅうはちにち) **ni-jū-hachi-nichi** the 28th
29日(にじゅうくにち) **ni-jū-ku-nichi** the 29th
30日(さんじゅうにち) **san-jū-nichi** the 30th
31日(さんじゅういちにち) **san-jū-ichi-nichi** the 31st

Minutes

1分(いっぷん) **ip-pun** one minute
2分(にふん) **ni-fun** two minutes
3分(さんぷん) **san-pun** three minutes
4分(よんぷん) **yon-pun** four minutes
5分(ごふん) **go-fun** five minutes
6分(ろっぷん) **rop-pun** six minutes
7分(ななふん) **nana-fun** seven minutes
8分(はちふん; はっぷん) **hachi-fun; hap-pun** eight minutes
9分(きゅうふん) **kyū-fun** nine minutes
10分(じっぷん) **jip-pun** ten minutes

Number of nights

1泊(いっぱく) **ip-paku** overnight stay
2泊(にはく) **ni-haku** two-night stay
3泊(さんぱく) **san-paku** three-night stay
4泊(よんはく) **yon-haku** four-night stay
5泊(ごはく) **go-haku** five-night stay
6泊(ろっぱく) **rop-paku** six-night stay
7泊(ななはく) **nana-haku** seven-night stay
8泊(はっぱく) **hap-paku** eight-night stay
9泊(きゅうはく) **kyū-haku** nine-night stay
10泊(じゅっぱく; じっぱく) **jup-paku; jip-paku** ten-night stay

Published by Tuttle Publishing, an imprint of Periplus Editions (Hong Kong) Ltd.

www.tuttlepublishing.com

This Revised and Expanded Edition
ISBN 978-4-8053-1398-5
ISBN 978-4-8053-1880-5 (for sale in Japan only)

Library of Congress Control Number:
2016955376

Distributed by

North America, Latin America & Europe
Tuttle Publishing
364 Innovation Drive, North Clarendon,
VT 05759-9436 U.S.A.
Tel: 1 (802) 773-8930; Fax: 1 (802) 773-6993
info@tuttlepublishing.com
www.tuttlepublishing.com

Asia Pacific
Berkeley Books Pte. Ltd.
3 Kallang Sector #04-01, Singapore 349278
Tel: (65) 6741-2178; Fax: (65) 6741-2179
inquiries@periplus.com.sg
www.tuttlepublishing.com

Japan
Tuttle Publishing
Yaekari Building, 3rd Floor, 5-4-12 Osaki
Shinagawa-ku, Tokyo 141 0032
Tel: (81) 3 5437-0171; Fax: (81) 3 5437-0755
sales@tuttle.co.jp
www.tuttle.co.jp

27 26 25 24   10 9 8 7 6   2404CM
Printed in China